PRAISE FOR
TRANSCENDENTAL
LEADERSHIP

"*Transcendental Leadership* takes you to the core of what leadership is about. Rather than providing outside remedies, Shawne Mitchell provides a pathway for the reader to connect with their own essence of being. So timely in our changing world, this book has taken me to places of understanding, stillness, and connection from which I have found myself able to lead with more focus, clarity, and impact."

PETER MATTHIES, CEO, Conscious Business Institute

"Shawne Mitchell's new book, *Transcendental Leadership*, is an empowering narrative offering guidance for today's leaders and change-makers to lead through a sense of deeper wisdom. Her book emphasizes the worldview that serving the whole is the only logical way forward in these times. Shawne presents a path forward for humans and all life on this planet we collectively call home. A book worth reading."

STEPHAN RECHTSCHAFFEN, M.D., author of *Timeshifting*, founder, Blue Spirit Retreat (Costa Rica), cofounder, The Omega Institute (New York)

"*Transcendental Leadership* is *the* new narrative for leaders during this time of transformation and shifting worldviews. Shawne captures the essence of discovering one's portals to accessing states of transcendence for leaders to thus be informed and guided in alignment with universal wisdom and compassionate engagement. She astutely amplifies the relationship between the 'being' and 'doing' of transcendence. Her writing is vibrant and conversational, offering rich examples from her own 'peek/peak' experiences and those of others."

JULIET ROHDE-BROWN, PH.D., clinical psychologist and Chair, Depth Psychology, Pacifica Graduate Institute

"In these topsy-turvy turbulent times, once again soul-based leadership is being called from our collective knowing. Now is the time to listen to your heart and mind, and read *Transcendental Leadership* to access portals and practices essential for leaders today."

BISHOP HEATHER SHEA, CEO and Spiritual Director, United Palace of Spiritual Arts (NYC)

"We are all called to our inner leadership to navigate our lives and be of greater service to humanity in these challenging times. In this book, Shawne has masterfully crafted a roadmap that we can all be inspired and guided by to claim our leadership. The book is filled with stories, wisdoms and solutions of how we can all move into our inner mastery."

AGAPI STASSINOPOULOS, author of *Wake Up to the Joy of You*

"This book feels like reading Plato's 'Allegory of the Cave' for the first time because it gives such a clear understanding of the variety of leadership energies and processes that exist and are intertwined. Making these mysterious processes 'visible' and describing them so subtly and vividly is of the utmost importance to the Phase Shift of Humanity, as it also prepares us to connect in various 'sexy' ways, and even more deeply, with the Great Universal Being, the Source and ourselves. Shawne Mitchell's book, as a self-contained portal to trans-cendence experiences, is a great resource to make us think."

ROBERT SCHRAM, cofounder, United Earth, director, Mother Earth Trust, transition engineer, WorldSummit and HackHumanity, host, Future Now Radio, and documentary film producer

"Shawne weaves together perspectives from some of the leaders in this world who are pointing the way towards the world we all deeply desire—a world with life-affirming relationships to each other and the rest of life on Earth."

PETER MERRY, PH.D., leadership expert, social entrepreneur, and philosopher

"Shawne shares the vision of a new leadership paradigm in which transformation of the *being* of a leader contributes to their wisdom and thusly, serving and supporting their endeavors. Her passion for researching portals and pathways to shift our individual and collective consciousness is reflected in every page of this book. We are fortunate because the principles and practices she shares could make it possible for us to uplift the consciousness in the world."

WILDRIK TIMMERMAN, cofounder, Mandali Retreat Center

"Shawne Mitchell's unique and inspiring narrative of leadership describes meaningful principles and practices leaders can use to take their capacities to the next level. It is all about accessing states of transcendence. She has cataloged known gateways that can provide leaders with increased awareness, spiritual presence, and universal wisdom."

PATTY DEDOMINIC, CEO, DeDominic & Associates

"In *Transcendental Leadership*, Shawne Mitchell takes us on an engaging journey that showcases practices known to sustain leaders cognitively, emotionally, and spiritually by supporting them to surpass ordinary states of being. In this way, they will be fully equipped to help us meet the greatest challenges of our time. A must-read for anyone that leads a group of any size."

DIANE MARIE WILLIAMS, founder,
The Source of Synergy Foundation

"Shawne's new book, *Transcendental Leadership*, is a lodestar for aspiring conscious leaders. Including examples from her own journey of transformation, she provides readers with pathways to a new form of conscious leadership—leading from an alignment with universal wisdom in service to our world. Well worth reading!"

PETER RUSSELL author of *Letting Go of Nothing*

"Transcendental Leadership is a great addition to the literature on conscious leadership. Shawne Mitchell does a superb job of providing value for the reader who aspires to lead more authentically and with greater mindfulness. A must-read for anyone in the leadership field."

JOHN RENESCH, award-winning author and futurist

"Transcending the apparent separateness of our world is likely the most vital and urgent task we have on personal and collective levels. *Transcendental Leadership* is an inspiring and practical guide to such inner and outer transcendence to experience the world as an innately interconnected whole. Crucially, it empowers leaders by giving them the framework of a holistic worldview based on the convergence of science and universal wisdom teachings in which to embody their evolutionary purpose so they may serve the good of the whole—benefiting both people and our planetary home."

JUDE CURRIVAN, PH.D., cosmologist, author of *The Cosmic Hologram,* and cofounder of WholeWorld-View

"A much-needed guide to ancient, deep wisdom for today's leaders in these chaotic and often confusing times."

CATHERINE BUTLER, founder, At the Chapel

"Beyond 'holistic leadership,' beyond 'transformational leadership,' even beyond 'visionary leadership,' author and entrepreneur Shawne Mitchell takes us to the next level: *transcendental leadership.* Her focus on the connection between

Source and management styles offers a unique perspective, intended to connect leaders with their spiritual essence. Beginning with an outline of the history of leadership, Shawne then identifies a collection of traits that distinguish transcendental leaders from others. Perhaps the most compelling aspect of her vision is her chapter on portals to transcendental leadership—including, for example, nature, movement, relationship, service, and devotion. I recommend this book for anyone interested in exploring the potentials for truly effective, heart-centered leadership—in any field of endeavor."

CHRISTIAN DE QUINCEY, PH.D., philosopher and author of *BlindSpots*

"*Transcendental Leadership* is an innovative guide showcasing principles and practices for accessing states of transcendence and evolving leadership to the next level. With these, the hope is that leaders will align with universal wisdom and develop their inner and outer awareness, opening them to the universal heart that serves as a compass."

ANNE-MARIE VOORHOEVE, founder, director, and strategic connector of the Hague Center (Netherlands)

"Shawne Mitchell has provided a gateway into what wisdom means in our turbulent and chaotic time. She has offered pearls of wisdom to guide us as we find our way into the future. This is a very important book."

JIM GARRISON, PH.D., President, Ubiquity University

"Accessing transcendent fields of energy and information, plus the capacity for storytelling, is an essential attribute for the twenty-first-century leader. Shawne's book, including the remarks of the transcendental leaders she interviewed, can help show you the way. Our world needs leadership imbued with new vision, inspiration, and passion."

ESPERIDE ANANAS AMETISTA, psychosociologist, writer, healer, and ambassador for Damanhur Spiritual Community

"Shawne Mitchell has provided us with an invaluable resource in *Transcendental Leadership*. Finally, in one place, one can find words of inspiring wisdom and practical advice from people who have learned how to express the Divine in their personal and professional lives. Shawne's book can help each of us in our transformational journey to become an authentic, loving self— and never has the world needed these lessons more than today."

STEPHEN CRONCOTA, former Chief Marketing Officer, Versace, and former Executive Vice President, Warner Bros. and Sony Pictures

"Shawne Mitchell's new book, *Transcendental Leadership*, is a wise and inspiring beacon for leaders wanting to connect with a spiritual influence, universal wisdom, and greater consciousness in their leadership capacities. I felt an energetic quality of the words on the page."

JUDI WEISBART, CEO, A Busy Woman Consulting

"We sit at the advent of a great shift in our collective journey. There exist crucibles in history when the conditions appear for a transformational age. An accumulation of people and ideas appear. Here is one. Leadership aligned with the transcendent universal wisdom of Source is a clarion call to the visionary leaders of the twenty-first century, those with an inner knowing that they want to contribute to and compassionately serve others and our planet. Shawne Mitchell's new book, *Transcendental Leadership,* offers guidance and eleven portals with which to inform and to lead from one's state of being instead of only from the state of busy doing. Her book is a beautiful gift to the world."

PARIS ACKRILL AND ROGER TEMPEST,
cofounders Avalon Wellbeing, Broughton Sanctuary

TRANSCENDENTAL LEADERSHIP

Ageless Principles and Practices for Leading in a Time of Awakening

SHAWNE MITCHELL

Foreword by Joseph Jaworski & Susan Taylor

SOUL STYLE PRESS
SANTA BARBARA, CALIFORNIA

Soul Style Press / Shawne Mitchell
www.ShawneMitchell.com
shawne@soulstyle.com

Transcendental Leadership / Shawne Mitchell
Library of Congress Control Number 2021917736
ISBN: 978-0-9889677-2-4 (paperback)

DEDICATION

This book is dedicated to my beloved sons,
Travis Mitchell Cook and Austin Richard Cook.
You guys are the best gifts of my life.

And to my brothers,
Christopher King Mitchell,
Frederick King Mitchell, Jr. (Mitch),
Ryan Kirkpatrick John Mitchell,
Daniel Rutherford Mitchell,
Richard Putnam Mitchell (deceased),
and their families:
I'm blessed and grateful for
our family tribe.

CONTENTS

CONTENTS

AUTHOR'S NOTE

A word about pronouns.

In this book, in order to avoid the awkward *he/she* and *him/her* sentence constructs and the masculine term *mankind,* I'm attempting—as much as possible—to use the pronouns *they* and *them* and the collective term *humanity.*

A word about names for Source.

I will primarily be using the terms *Source* and *Universal Wisdom* for the following names attributed to the concept/construct of God: Spirit, Universe, the Divine, Ground of Being, True Nature, Buddha Nature, and the One Mind.

Defining the term *awake.*

What do I mean by the concept of awakening? In the context of our conversation in this book, I define awakening as emerging from the deep sleep of unconscious living. To awaken from the slumber of the inner soul-self within each of us. To inquire, explore, and discover what is truly meaningful and important, not only to ourselves, but also to others and, in fact, our whole planet.

FOREWORD

Joseph Jaworski and Susan Taylor,
Cofounders of Generon International

Over the past decade, our world has been facing profound change and rising complexity, increasing at a scale, intensity, and speed never experienced before. Then came 2020, an unprecedented, turbulent year that will remain in our minds and hearts for generations to come, given its world-shifting events. From a deadly pandemic to a global movement for racial justice, our daily lives became that of face masks, hand sanitizer, lockdowns, unemployment, violent protests, devastating wildfires, murder hornets, massive flooding, extreme weather events, political unrest, covid-19 vaccines, and the Dow Jones industrial average suffering its worst single-day point drop ever. Life became more strenuous and stressful. So many have suffered economically and socially for reasons that include unemployment, home destruction, and tremendous loss of human life.

And the future forecasts more of the same.

"It is often that we taste the darkness of death before we can rise with the strength and courage we did not even know we had until it was tested." —Unknown

From the ideas of John W. Gardner, we have learned that nothing is truly ever safe. Every meaningful battle must be fought and re-fought. He said, "We need to develop a resilient, indomitable morale that enables us to face those realities and still strive with every ounce of energy to prevail."[1]

The world has broken open in so many ways. Maybe you're wondering if such a struggle and this seemingly endless uncertainty isn't more than human beings can bear. Yet all of history suggests that the human spirit is well fitted to cope with just this kind of world—a notion that feels both frightening and exciting!

The year 2020 was traumatic; make no mistake. At the same time, the year and its aftermath reshaped us through its many gifts. Resilience, collaboration, connection, empathy, courage, and self-discovery to name a few. Perhaps we are now in a space in between the old and the new where uncertainty and ambiguity are not just abundant but tend to thrive as we realize our new skills. Design innovative processes. Reimagine solutions and outcomes. More deeply understand what it means to be alone together. Grieve. Heal. And discover that technology is not the enemy of humanity. This is an opportunity to reexamine our personal commitment to renewal—cocreating new understandings—as we take our individual and collective stand on how we want to answer the call of our time.

As the very foundations of our world continue to be transformed from more stable to dynamic patterns, the nature of leadership must change as well. To succeed in this new environment, leaders must pay attention to their tacit source of knowledge, becoming living examples of what is possible and creating new realities as they enable the emergence of a more comprehensive worldview and a belief system adequate for civilization to rise above its current challenges.

But where do we go from here? What are the implications for the contribution and benefits of transcendental leadership to the governance of organizations and all sectors of our society?

We are on the threshold of awakening to a level of consciousness in which all human beings recognize they are one with Source. Shawne Mitchell's book *Transcendental Leadership* explores this realization in the context of leadership.

Shawne has interviewed over twenty-five transcendental leaders leading organizations today who have provided insights and stories about their efforts at leading from transcendence—in some cases for decades—describing specific practices and intentions they use to guide their organizations and institutions. From all of these dialogs, one thing is clear: Leaders who acknowledge their *knowing* relationship with Source have a compelling *being* that informs their choices and actions, exhibiting a capacity for extraordinary functioning and performance. This book shows the reader how to activate their being in order to access universal wisdom, elevate their vibrational presence, and serve the whole for the benefit of all.

New to the literature on leadership are the *portals* to transcendence Shawne has identified from her research and her catalog of practices leaders can utilize to achieve alignment with Source, regulating their states of being. The portals are universally human, found in every culture worldwide.

Leadership theory has undergone an evolution in recent years and, without throwing away anything valuable, this is the next iteration beyond mindfulness. Shawne offers a cross-cultural survey of transcendence practices that come from Buddhism, Christianity, Judaism, Islam, Hinduism, and Indigenous wisdom. The practices that she documents are both ancient and contemporary.

Of course, everyone must determine the portals and practices that resonate with them as an individual. Nobody can dictate this for another.

In this same connection, the most critical transcendental leadership *trait* is the capacity for *deep inner listening*—that place where courage and commitment meet to allow our wholeness to emerge—light and shadow—through curiosity and without judgment, as we willingly listen to and discover all parts of ourselves through an openness to learn, to receive, to awaken and to share. It is only through deep inner listening that we enable ourselves to tap into the implicate order of the cosmos, allowing the presence of Source to inform our being, which in turn informs our leadership.

Susan Taylor often reminds us that the words *listen* and *silent* contain the same letters. Silence is the essence to deep inner listening, which most of us feel challenged to practice, given our always-on 24/7 mentality along with our overstimulated minds and under-stimulated senses. Yet silence is available to everyone. The indigenous peoples knew this; they practiced deep listening as a spiritual skill to cultivate inner, quiet still awareness.

We are in a moment of great peril and great promise. Leaders must live and act in the hope that beckons from beyond the conventional. It was Socrates who said: "Know thyself." It was Generon's former business partner, Bill O'Brien, who said: "The success of any intervention is dependent upon the interior condition of the intervenor."

Yet because of our obsessions with our leaders, we forget that, in its essence, leadership is about learning how to shape the future. Leadership exists when people are no longer victims of circumstances but instead *participate in creating new circumstances*. Ultimately, leadership is about creating new realities.

Who you are has a direct impact upon what you create and how you lead. Acts of leadership therefore cannot be separated from the identity and integrity of oneself. A deeper understanding of self is vital toward creating the new realities required to sustain our future.

Joseph Jaworski speaks to this by sharing the story of his father, Leon Jaworski, who became a special prosecutor during the Watergate Scandal. During the disturbing investigation, Joseph and his father asked each other the same question the nation would soon ask: *"How could this have happened amongst our highest and most trusted officials?"* It was from this inquiry that Joseph committed to bring forth a new generation of leadership. It is from a similar inquiry that Shawne shares the ageless principles and practices for leading in a time of awakening.

Transcendental Leadership is the new, emerging narrative for leaders during this time of transformation along with the practical applications they will need to consciously lead during this critical, evolutionary time.

Joseph Jaworski
September 6, 2021
Wimberley, Texas

Susan Taylor
September 6, 2021
Hilton Head, South Carolina

PREFACE

I came to write this book because of my interest in the adventures of the spirit. All my life, I have had a boundless curiosity about the unseen and timeless mystery at the heart of everyone's life journey. The mystery of the spiritual.

Humanity is awakening. It's my intention with this book to provide a new, emerging model and narrative of leadership— *transcendental leadership*—along with a set of principles and practices for leading during this critical, evolutionary time. As far as I know, this book is a unique treatise on leadership, one focused on *how* leaders can access states of transcendence that inherently cultivate their *being*, allowing it to inform their internal disposition and worldview. By aligning *who* they already are and what they *do now* with the Source of universal wisdom and present awareness, they are serving the whole.

Inculcating our being with holy states of transcendent, universal wisdom is an important, even essential, goal, because what humanity needs today—on a global scale—are leaders whose actions are holistic. There is no avoiding the interconnectivity of global economics, business, and politics on our people's wellbeing and the environment anymore or denying the enduring effect of the human presence everywhere we live. And I believe that we have come to realize, fundamentally, that where we place our attention/intention begets our unfolding reality.

In this book, it is assumed that the natural intention and innate desire of each of us is to remember ourselves—to integrate our spirits and physical beings—and in this way, to come home to Source.

We are in an opportunity vector brought on by several cooccurring crises—not just the covid-19 pandemic, but what it is bringing to our immediate attention. To change humanity's course to survive and take advantage of these openings requires us to adopt a new measure of consciousness for each other and the planet. We need leaders who have a heightened sense of self- and other-awareness, who are guided by their connection to universal wisdom and understand that their innate being is the guiding light to leading others. We need them to embrace a must-do-something-now sensibility.

I came to write this book because of my interest in having adventures of the spirit and because I believe that changes which could make a real difference in meeting the needs of our era and of our planet are to be found in the transformation of our hearts, the development of our conscious awareness, and our understanding that we are all connected.

What Brought This About?

I love to travel. There is something about the unknown that I have always been curious about: unknown locales, undiscovered cultures, and unmet people that yield in me some kind of heightened awareness. Plus, I have always been curious about the spiritual, mysterious unknown and unseen realms. The curiosity of the unknown raises my vibration. My psyche gets excited by experiencing the array of life on our extraordinary pearl of a planet!

I probably caught the travel bug when one of my older brothers went to Europe during college and then joined the Peace Corps after he graduated. I was about fourteen years old. I thought to myself, *Wow, that's really possible!* My curiosity was piqued.

By the time I was out of college, I was an avid practitioner of Transcendental Meditation (TM) and had been to Europe and North Africa a couple of times, going from country to country with my longtime friend Dianne, impulsively asking each other from day to day, "What's next? Where shall we go now?" and meditating. Unknowingly, I was seamlessly blending deep inner experiences with the richness of our outer adventures. There are a zillion stories in those months of travel and adventure for a couple of college girls from Bellevue, Washington.

Along with increasing curiosity and deeper inquiry, a confident explorer emerged in me when, after graduating from the University of Washington in Seattle with a bachelor's degree in communications, I got an offer to go to Brazil and work at the Brazilian National Institute of Space Research in Sao Jose dos Campos, midway between Sao Paolo and Rio de Janeiro, which at the time was a small town. Surprisingly, my parents were actually okay with this plan and supportive about me going off to Brazil by myself at age twenty-three. I packed up and off I went, alone and not speaking Portuguese.

Trust me here, this was *way* before we had the communications technologies of today. This was still the era of teletype, telephones, and written letters. Compared to now, communicating with a country on the other side of the planet in any kind of timely fashion was nearly impossible. I was on my own. When I look back on it now, I can hardly believe that I just up and went. Was I naïve?

Maybe. But I had the capacity and intuitive ability to sense any red flags, and to let whatever unfold day by day, from present moment to present moment.

Clearly, I could list the numerous obstacles, challenges, and potentially horrific possibilities that could have occurred. But guess what? Not a one did. Except that I became quite ill within the first few weeks with dysentery, perhaps due to a parasitic invasion, and suffered about a billion mosquito bites.

I recovered.

All that being said, the spirit of global exploration and adventure became thoroughly entrenched into my body, mind, heart, and soul in Brazil. In addition, I experienced a tremendous amount of solitude, such that, through my meditation practice, I also began to discover the spiritual gems to be found spelunking the caves deep within my inner being. And *there* is where I found the adventures of the Spirit.

It was *there* too that I discovered that *I* was the leader of my life, *I* was the leader of my soul, *I* was the leader of how I might manifest my personal reality. And that this "I" was not just the Shawne I, it/I was also the *I Am*. Source. Divinity. The One Mind.

From this, I began grokking frequent numinous experiences, such as the capacity to sense, feel, and perceive the energy of a field of grace and the luminous presence of Source.

The deep inner knowing acquired in Brazil was so profound for me that it has compelled me to this very day to share with others that this connection and alignment is available to everyone. I feel it is imperative that every individual, most especially those that want to be leaders in today's world, needs to plumb the spiritual depths within themselves.

The presence of Source and transcendent awareness is in every person and in every*thing*. When you think about it, it can't *not* be.

Our leaders need to discover their personal portals to transcendence, discerning which practices provide for them the being, frequency, traits, and characteristics necessary to lead our world in the twenty-first century and beyond—especially due to the seriousness of the challenges we are currently facing.

The field of leadership often overlooks the most vital capacity required for our time in history: accessing transcendent states of awareness. The word *transcendence* contains the Latin prefix *trans,* meaning "beyond," and the root verb *scandare,* meaning "to climb." In brief, then, *to transcend* means to surpass normal human experience, to experience the numinous, the sacred; to enter the spiritual realm; to perceive the nature of consciousness.

Transcendental leadership employs this perception. Not only in a personal way, but also in a business or organizational context. It differs from other models of leadership because its foundation is the recognition that we live in an orderly and conscious universe where we are innately connected to the Source of all things.

Ancient wisdom from cultures around the world asserts that at the basis of all consciousness is the Ground of Being—also known as Source, God, and other names devised by the people of different ages and cultures. Because of this recognition, transcendental leadership is both an inner path of self-discovery and an outer path that can teach individuals, organizations, and society at large to engage in new world views and perceptions, and to think and act more holistically.

This model of leadership is a marriage between leadership and the philosophy of transcendence blended from our known spiritual traditions, transpersonal psychology, and the interconnectivity of fields of coherence.

This book grew out of my master's thesis for a degree in consciousness studies at the University of Philosophical Research in Los Angeles. In conducting research on relevant concepts, I studied the literature of diverse religious and spiritual traditions, looking for clues as to the nature of consciousness and the oneness of all beings in relationship to leadership. I researched philosophy from fragments of early Greek texts and classic works of literature by thinkers and authors ranging from Heraclitus and Plato in antiquity to nineteenth-century American philosopher Ralph Waldo Emerson, founder of the Transcendentalist Movement. I was looking for references to the nature of Source or the One Mind, transcendent experience, and leadership. And I looked for references both in the context of self-leadership and in the context of possessing the qualities and traits necessary for being a leader of others.

In the essay "Illusions," Emerson writes:

> *Whatever games are played with us, we must play no games with ourselves, but deal in our privacy with the last honesty and truth. This reality is the foundation of friendship, religion, poetry, and art. At the top or at the bottom of all illusions, I set the cheat which still leads us to work and live for appearances. In spite of our conviction, in all sane hours, it is what we really are that avails with friends, with strangers, and with fate or fortune.*[1]

What Emerson is referring to when he says, "We must play no games with ourselves but deal in our privacy (inner self) with honesty and truth" is personal authenticity—a key trait of transcendental leadership. Indeed, this is the foundation of a life lived with integrity.

Where he says, "It is what we are that avails with friends, with strangers, and with fate or fortune," he is telling us that it is *who* we are—meaning, who we are *being* as we walk through the world, including in our personal lives—that puts us in a position to lead others.

We earn the right to lead by showing up as a person of integrity—someone honest, authentic, compassionate, and transparent.

Many people have come to the realization that whatever humankind is doing to secure our future isn't working. Most of us feel disillusioned with our leaders, mistrustful of our governments and institutions, and increasingly despondent about this state of affairs. Our collective behavior and our cultural and economic structures do not satisfy our basic inner needs for meaning, happiness, contribution, and peaceful wellbeing. For this, we must explore transcendence.

Transcendence is an element of the human experience that diminishes our sense of separateness from other people and the rest of nature. Leading from a place of transcendence and authenticity—being deeply genuine and transparent—is critically important because, not only does the future of our planet depend on increasing the level of authentic communication among people, but humanity's wellbeing depends on our coming to the mutual realization of our interrelatedness with all other species on Earth.

Some of the best-selling books of our era are about humanity's search for meaning, personal wellbeing, and spiritual truth. There is a smorgasbord of information available to us on topics of psychotherapy, self-help, ecospirituality, and mysticism to breakthroughs in the sciences of physics, biology, consciousness studies, chemistry, and neurobiology that could help advance the evolution of consciousness and the causes of global social and spiritual connection. I believe that as more individuals are transformed by their exposure to universal wisdom and, additionally, practice applying ageless principles in their lives, the organizations and communities to which they belong will be transformed for the better. It is the inner experience of the wisdom in our own lives that transforms us, and by extension, impacts our worldview. Truly wise leaders have the ability to influence corporations, institutions, businesses, and communities around the world to do the same.

My conclusion is that an evolving leadership of transcendence needs to be at the forefront if we are to survive our current challenges.

There is an element of personal responsibility that transcendental leaders accept. People in greater numbers than ever before are becoming aware of the fact that we have been collectively allowing massive injustices to occur on a global scale. We are in a new era where we are no longer willing to stand in silence and acquiesce to the systematic oppression of those in control. Injustice has insidiously infiltrated our systems of business, governance, and institutions (especially those associated with privilege). The United States, among obvious other countries, has been enculturated by ideologies we would never have agreed to intentionally if we had been awake to the underlying greed at the core of the activities being orchestrated in our names from behind the scenes.

As I write, we are in the midst of a global pandemic and worldwide economic injustices and disparity are rampant. Despite evidence of the inequities of race and economic class, however, members of the American government are insidiously passing all kinds of legislation to revoke and end progressive initiatives and laws. It is happening virtually "behind our backs" primarily because the corporate media has the populace focused on other matters, like a few billionaires racing to space, unemployment, the decision of whether or not to vaccinate, and the continuously evolving virus variants that threaten to kill millions over the next few years. People in power are using this moment in history to be opportunistic to their personal greed and the self-interests of their cronies.

This is seriously wrong. Leaders in our political community, who are supposed to be our representatives, no longer act as if they represent the people of the country. Instead, they follow the money to corporations, lobbyists, and self-interests (as opposed to public interests) at all costs. These leaders are operating from the fear-based mentality and emotions of separation and "not enough."

Of necessity, most people choose not to understand and know themselves well, remaining detached from their authentic selves. We are purposely inundated by innumerable distractions. We are so overwhelmed that we are basically trained not to pause, question, or go within; not to trust our inner selves; not to take stock and detach from our ever-present doing, doing, doing. Our distraction with surviving has resulted in the dismantling and transformation of the U.S. government of the people, by the people, for the people to a government of a few of the people, by a few of the people, for a few of the people. This did not occur overnight. As the U.S. population was being lulled into complacency and distraction, leaders, who are allied with big business, set up systems that siphon huge portions of material wealth and control into the hands of a very few.

It's important to note that this is not strictly a phenomenon in the United States but in many countries (both the so-called developed nations and those that are not) around the entire world. Many of the countries in the world are distracted by their insidious, horrific wars and political leadership.

Those in charge of organizations and institutions need the transformative values, insight, and awakened leadership as exemplified by the self-aware leader grounded in a paradigm-shifting model of transcendental leadership, because—like it or not—the corporate world may be the most important lever we have for making necessary change in the world today. Solutions often need to align with financial incentives.

The most powerful leaders in the world have slowly and surely manifested a structure that causes most of humanity to feel anxious, frightened, hopeless, and disconnected. Our society ignores the cries of endangered creatures, shows disrespect towards the plant kingdom, and expresses a dismissive attitude towards our climate catastrophe and the worldwide depletion of natural resources, putting all life at risk. As a species, we have pretty much screwed things up for Mother Nature and Planet Earth.

Ours is a time of reckoning, of facing ourselves and all the creations and institutions and systems that we have either built or acquiesced to others to construct that are alienating us from each other. By blindly allowing individuals in powerful positions to siphon off the economic wellbeing of the vast majority of people and to rule by propagating fear and separation, we have been silently complicit. But the transformative awareness of a new narrative of leadership is available. It is one that can help us (paraphrasing Ken Wilber) to wake up, grow up, clean up, open up, and show up to transform our world.[2]

Transcendental leadership and transcendence itself will help us to free ourselves from corrupt systems of control because these systems cannot align to the higher frequencies of Source, as love, compassion, and inclusion are its inherent nature.

Now is the season to know
That everything you do
Is sacred.[3]
—Hafiz

INTRODUCTION

*Leading from a connection and relationship with the
transcendent is a truth meant for the blessing and upliftment of
humanity and respect for the wellbeing and soul of our planet.*

Today, our world is increasingly fast-paced and complex. Also, with
the advances in technology and the level of chaotic change
technology is producing in nations around the world, even the
most emotionally stable individuals often feel overwhelmed. We
need to broaden our perspective and worldview to account for the
uncertainty we will continue to experience. In this small book, I can
only showcase an introductory glimpse of what I would call my
intuitively perceived interpretation of the current models of
leadership, the ancient and spiritual philosophies and scriptural
writings conscientiously studied for their attunements to soul-
awakened leadership and conscious awareness, and our modern
understanding of the intricate unity and interconnectedness of all
life. Leading from a connection and relationship with the
transcendent is a truth meant for the blessing and upliftment of
humanity and respect for the wellbeing and soul of our planet.

Fortunately, people are beginning to embrace a worldview that
combines ancient ways of knowing and being with contemporary
knowledge and awareness of global interconnection. In my
opinion, this evolving worldview is necessary if we are to sustain
our species and maintain the integrity of our beautiful home

planet. Among other things, it will help us to be better stewards of Earth and its resources.

Why is remembering ancient knowledge relevant to contemporary leadership and the survival of life on Earth? Our planet, never mind our entire universe, is not the chance result of a fortuitous combination of gases, subatomic particles, and unknown forces that the material scientists have long proposed. How, can you imagine, did various energetic forces, gases, and particles harmoniously coalesce to provide an environment that has created systems of life evolving into sentient beings? I don't believe that it's random coincidences and blind forces which are adept at organizing the minutiae required for the miraculous creation of life, let alone, how a single microscopic cell can spring into human intelligence. How arrogant and obtuse can we be not to humbly drop to our knees?

The Nature of Transcendence

Transcendence is a concept with definitions ranging from the philosophical and theological to the spiritual and experiential. It is often described as an inner spiritual experience of awakening to your metaphysical essence. This experience has been expounded upon in the ancient sacred literature of every wisdom tradition around the world, including *The Bhagavad Gita* (compiled between 500–200 B.C.E.) and *The Yoga Sutras of Patanjali* (400 B.C.E.) in the East, and *The Bible* (compiled between 300 B.C.E. and 1600 C.E.) in the West.

The important reason why transcendence is so highly prized by those privileged to experience it is that it dramatically shifts our self-identity *(our being)* resulting in a more enlightened change of our actions *(our doing)*.

Transcendental leadership is leadership that embraces the spiritual dimension of our lives, which includes inner transformation and self-realization. Its purpose is to assist individuals, businesses, organizations, governments, and institutions devoted to education, health, sustainability, and economic equality to evolve and elevate their individual and collective mindset, behaviors, and activities. As influential leaders shift the mindsets of their followers on a global scale, our communities, society, and organizations will also evolve, thrive, and focus on serving the whole.

Mass awakening can only start with individual awakening because each of us is the leader of our own life. But none of us is alone. Each of us—man, woman, nonbinary individual, and child—is connected to the rest of humankind on an energetic level. All life on Earth is unified in one massive ecosystem shielded from outer space by the bubble of our atmosphere. Plus, we and the entire cosmos are also aspects of one quantum field.

The beauty of recognizing how unified we are with one another and all life on Earth is that when we awaken to our inner reality in the knowledge of the self-divine within us, as an individual, our "exterior" reality begins to shift and our consciousness expands. Our being reflects upon and informs the world around us.

When I think of transcendental leadership, I am reminded of an experience I had being a participating journalist in a race in Madagascar in 1993. The Raid Gauloises, as it was called, was an international, extreme orienteering race, the precursor to what became the Eco-Challenge in the United States. This was a

Survivor-type experience that, at the time, took place each year in remote regions of the world. Yes, off I went alone: following thirty-five race teams from all over the world for two weeks, while carrying my own backpack, tent, food, and water. Living in the remote island outback, each and every unique-unto-itself day and night can only be described as harrowing, foolish, extraordinary, exhilarating, and challenging. Yet, countless times, I also had luminous and numinous peek/peak experiences of inner and outer illumination, spiritual connection to unseen forces, and unexpected and intimate experiences of coherence with the other journalists, race participants, and, in a few cases, the local people. Sometimes these occurred when I was alone and sometimes when I was immersed in a community of strangers on a foreign and wild island in the Indian Ocean.

Although at the time I didn't realize it, I had accumulated four important skills and assets that would support me on this once-in-a-life-time experience: many years of a meditation practice, an athletic and strong body, social skills to navigate with others speaking in languages other than my own, and an adventurous confidence built up from years of travel in both first-world and third-world environments. In particular, my longtime meditation practice provided me with emotional balance, a calm and centered inner strength, intuitive sensibilities, and trust—both of myself and others.

I had a number transcendent-like epiphanies during the Raid. Among them was my discovery that when performing very challenging tasks, whether operating as an individual or as a member of a team, time appeared to slow down and the group would perform together as if from a single intelligence—without linear thinking or direction. This is the state I will refer to throughout this book as *coherence*. It is frequently found in Indigenous groups.

Also, there were times of intense focus when I was embodied by a deeper level of knowing, such that, as needed, internal resources like endurance, courage, resilience, patience, and compassion surfaced spontaneously.

External resources always manifested as needed too.

Examples of my personal realization and development were playing full out, so I was capable of being autonomously self-reliant, though still knowing when it was necessary to ask for help.

A major realization of mine was that a team is only as strong as its weakest member. The Navy Seal guys on the U.S. team, while supercompetitive men, left their egos at the door when they were in the bush together. They were always aware of each other's wellbeing and would seamlessly exchange roles as leaders when warranted.

All in all, in my soul, I knew that these two weeks on my own in the extraordinary wilds of Madagascar, would inform and shape my thinking and behavior for the rest of my life.

Through the guiding principles of transcendental leadership, it is my role to facilitate an expansion of the consciousness of the individuals who create the strategies, practices, and systems of the larger framework of organizations in which I participate or provide consulting. In turn, this has the potential to transform the larger framework of the entire shared day-to-day reality of all beings on the planet, which contributes to the wellbeing and sustainability of our planet.

Transcendental Leadership Evolves Us

As I began my research, I found hundreds of contemporary studies, books, and articles on different elements of leadership. Many of those who write on, speak about, and teach leadership agree that self-knowledge is a fundamental building block of effective leadership, but very few say that a basic characteristic of effective leadership is possessing a spiritual ethic. The notion of self-knowledge among leaders predominantly relates to personality traits, such as your skills, talents, and aptitudes. Rarely do courses on building leadership skills encourage individuals to undergo rigorous self-inquiry. Nor do they teach or encourage learning about the deeper dimensions of the human experience that are typically accessed only through activities like silence, contemplation, meditation, solitude in nature, those portals to awakening and transformation that represent largely unexplored territory in traditional leadership and management theory and practice.

At its essence, transcendental leadership is an approach to life and work—*a way of being*—that has the potential to create positive change everywhere throughout our society. Imagine leaders *leading from a place of transcendence.* Imagine leading from this perspective yourself! It is a style of leadership that represents a radical, and yet hopeful, attempt to synthesize leading-edge, openminded critical thinking with the tenets of ancient wisdom and ethics, and tools for awakening consciousness, such as meditation to effect profound collective change. Awakening practices by definition are those that open the portals to transcendent experiences.

Awakened and awakening individuals from many different fields and organizations recognize the same principles and practices of transcendence as valuable to leadership. Transcendental leadership synthesizes personal skills such as deep, personal honesty and rigorous critical thinking with a willingness to explore living systems, the Implicate Order of the universe, and the fields of energy that connect individual beings and the entire cosmos.

Transcendental leadership is the new narrative we should endorse. Becoming a transcendental leader is the journey of awakening your *already-present knowing* so you may lead others both by example and by how you express your energy—your alignment with Source.

This book is meant to be short and relatively concise in order that you, dear reader, may raise your frequency of being and develop your capacity to access states of transcendence by quickly grasping the principles and practices that will attune you to your highest self. The foundational element of this capacity stems from your *being,* not just from your doing.

There are five short chapters in this book, with reflections and/or an exercise at the end of each, plus an epilogue, and biographical details of my interview subjects.

In Chapter 1, "A *Very* Brief History of Leadership Styles," I share historical theories of leadership in the West, as well, as some that are more recent, such as the concepts of mindful leadership and conscious leadership. Acknowledging early models of leadership and the progression of leadership theory is foundational to comprehending the evolutionary mindset of humanity. We will briefly review models such as the great man theory, transactional and behavioral theory, the patriarchal notion of *power-over*, and the popular model of servant leadership.

Chapter 2, "Transcendence and Wisdom in Leadership," provides the foundational principles/elements of the model of transcendental leadership that is postulated in this book which originated in my research and graduate studies. It begins with a description of profound philosophical wisdom from known great thinkers. From ancient Greece to today—linking their teachings on states of transcendence with leadership. A second principle researched are the primary spiritual-wisdom traditions known to humanity, including scriptural and time-honored teachings from their sacred writings, including (what we may know) of historic individuals considered to be spiritual masters, plus Indigenous wisdom passed down through the ages—all interfacing with— what I am calling Source, aligned with leading and leadership.

The third major principle brings modern science and quantum theory into the fold: blending what we now understand of the nature of reality, quantum science regarding the unifying and connective structure of the cosmos (as we know it), neurobiology, and the study of the nature of consciousness.

Chapter 3, "Traits of the Transcendental Leader," furnishes you with the traits and characteristics that the transcendental leader embodies, a coalescence of their *being* and compelling presence. I'm reminded to share that this book is not intended to provide you with a list and instruction on how to acquire the hard skills necessary to oversee and lead an organization efficiently and effectively, like forecasting, budgeting, strategy, time management, and marketing. No, I'm talking about the deep, "soft" skills, such as integrity, authenticity, the capacity to suspend, emotional balance and intelligence, creativity, intuition, and more.

Chapter 4, "Portals to Being a Transcendental Leader," explains the eleven primary portals through which spiritually masterful leaders access transcendent states. From my research, this chapter provides information I have not found in articles and other books on transcendental leadership. The heart of this style of leadership is *aligning with* Source and being *informed by* Source. Here I try to answer the questions: What are the *known* practices that—with intention, commitment, consistent practice, humility, and surrender—elevate your heart, mind, body, and soul—opening your connection and bringing you into alignment with Source. How may leaders blend universal wisdom, deep presence, and profound awareness with their passion and the purpose of serving?

You'll have the opportunity to learn about each portal of transcendental leadership and to explore which one, two, or three are your *primary* portals. You may discover that you resonate with many of the practices. However, for the purpose of deepening our alignment with Source, one or two will suffice. A sincere, deep, regular practice is the main thing required for the true fruits of transcendence to blossom and unfold in you and to enhance your leadership.

If you are already curious to know the categories of portals that exist, here you go: They are nature, meditation and contemplation, movement, creativity, relationship, devotion, inspired writings, service, knowing, Indigenous wisdom, and yoga.

The final chapter, Chapter 5, "Transcendental Leadership in Action Today," showcases and highlights living individuals—people with their feet on the ground, so to speak—whose being exemplifies the traits of transcendental leadership. I conducted personal interviews with most of these people. Some filled out a questionnaire. Some wrote essays both long and short, which were edited in most cases for the sake of brevity. Some met me for lengthy Zoom calls. *All* were kind enough to share their personal thoughts, stories, and notions of transcendental leadership in their work and lives today. It's my heartfelt hope that you will see yourself in some of these individuals, who, like you and me, want to lead lives of meaning and contribution to the wellbeing of others and our planet.

The Epilogue "Where Can We Go from Here?" addresses the implications and benefits of transcendental leadership in uplifting and serving all manner of leaders in our world today.

I

A *VERY* BRIEF HISTORY
OF LEADERSHIP

*We are experiencing an evolution in consciousness that is
rooted in a planetary worldview and birthing a
holographic vision of leadership which aligns heart, mind,
body, and soul for the good of all.*

From the beginning of recorded history, historians and
philosophers have explored the question: What qualities
distinguish an individual as a leader?

In Plato's time, the Sophists ruled Athens. Fourth-century
B.C.E. Athens was under their intellectual, political, social, and
economic influence. These teachers of philosophy (whose name
is derived from the Greek root for "wisdom," *sophos)* were paid
to educate members of the elite in the art of persuasive rhetoric.
Their legacy today is an association with deceptive reasoning. If
we call someone a sophist, we are saying that they are skillful at
making clever but false arguments.[1]

In *The Republic,* Plato addresses the selection and training of the leaders of Athens. He says that good leaders would be lovers of wisdom, devoted as much to pursuing the vision of truth as they are to the execution of governmental affairs. They are people that pursue the good above all other goals.

Leaders must be educated, according to Plato, but not just by injecting new knowledge into their minds. He advocated for them to sit silently and look deeply within themselves, seeking the source of wisdom. His words are these:

> *The philosopher whose dealings are with divine order himself acquires the characteristics of order and divinity...*[2]

From my point of view, Plato was describing the value of transcendental practices—of sitting silently and deeply reflecting within oneself in order to understand one's true nature and to align with Source.

Leadership development is human development. Leadership is often defined as the process in which one individual influences a group of individuals to attain a common goal. The goal is then, hopefully, attained by mutual cooperation and cohesive behavior. It is understood that a leader is someone who is committed to their cause. The leader takes responsibility for moving the cause forward and motivating and inspiring their followers to pursue the cause.

In addition to this commitment, transcendental leaders imbue their work with an authentic, positive attitude. They possess an abiding sense of self-esteem. Ideally, they continue to self-actualize through seeking out progressive leadership training and opportunities for personal/spiritual life growth to increase their self-awareness and their *being* as an exemplary individual and role model for those they lead. *This is the conscious individual's lifetime journey.*

Organizational theorists who have studied a variety of leaders have observed that those who are most effective tend to share the following traits. They:

- Are able to gain the trust and confidence of their followers through their *being* and style of communication.
- Have the ability to expeditiously make and execute difficult decisions.
- Work closely with their teams, and the welfare of their teams is their primary objective.
- Possess a strong moral compass, integrity, intelligence, flexibility, openness to experience, and conscientiousness.

These are things contemporary business schools teach future business leaders to do, along with developing the skills and mindset of management. Schools teach human psychology in an effort to help leaders find the best formula to get things done expeditiously in their organizations and be profitable. Management is customarily studied in the context of commerce; and what is deemed "success" in our contemporary world is financial success—a positive ROI.

From history, we can see that leaders evolve with the social mores of their eras. You would agree, I'm sure, that people's thinking and behavior is usually aligned with the collective thinking of the time. For the most part, our current beliefs and practices are still built upon the foundation of older ideas. Their lingering effect on our collective psyche needs to be brought up to date with new values and structures that are less biased and exclusionary. For example, we must have leaders that want their organizations to be diverse, conscious, inclusive, sustainable, and regenerative.

Executives primarily focused on financial success will be happy to know that studies show that diversity and inclusivity create more productive and profitable organizations, businesses, and industries. If you are reading this, I'm sure you are already aware of the newest acronym in human resources, the JEDI path of hiring, which is aiming to achieve justice, equality, diversity, and inclusivity.

In this chapter, we'll do a quick review and see what, if anything, of value emerged from the past models and theories of leadership that can inform our current discussion of bringing practices of transcendental awareness and transformation into the fold with other disciplines.

Before we do that, I feel that it's imperative to provide you with a short synopsis of at least a few of the major models from which the new evolutionary narrative of transcendental leadership derives. Let us begin.

The Trait Theory and the "Great Man" Model of Leadership

An early assumption in the study of leadership was that leadership is based solely on characteristics certain individuals possess. This notion, that individual attributes set leaders apart, became known as the *trait theory of leadership.*

Trait theory was explored at length in many works in the nineteenth century. In *Heroes, Hero-Worship, and the Heroic in History,* written in 1841, Scottish historian Thomas Carlyle studied and identified the attributes, talents, skills, and physical characteristics of history's great leaders. (It should be noted that all the leaders he studied were men). It was his assertion that great leaders were born natural leaders.

To add to this theory, British statistician Francis Galton's *Hereditary Genius,* written in 1869, examined leadership qualities in the families of powerful men, seeking to prove a genetic link to the greatness of these individuals. His studies provided the initial support for the theory that leadership was an inherited, biological trait.

Both of these nineteenth-century theorists assumed that people must be naturally gifted at birth with attributes which would make them quality leaders. They did not accept that skills could be learned. And one of the supposedly required traits of a leader was masculinity. Our culture is still struggling to overcome the inadequacy of this supposition.

There are many wonderful new books, groups, movements, and organizations that address the principles and attributes of what are called feminine qualities in leadership. It's an important and critical evolution to bring the yin (feminine energy) and the yang (masculine energy) together in leadership. In the East, yin and yang are complementary opposites. Neither exists on its own. Both are necessary.

The great man theory and the phrase *great man* emerged within the patriarchal institutions of the world's dominant monotheistic religions, Judaism, Islam, and Christianity, which went to great lengths to diminish and eradicate the role of women in their midst as leaders; and similarly, within the patriarchal hierarchies of governments and the militaries of powerful empires that were led by dynamic and often charismatic men. Although, the historical element of this theory became ingrained in our collective psyche and is still predominant in the twenty-first century, women are making inroads as leaders around the world. And, as we know, the current statistical research shows that women-led organizations "are more profitable, perform better, and have higher profit margins compared to male-led companies. When women lead, firms report that these economic benefits translate into profits of up to $1.8 billion globally."[3]

If you look back at leaders throughout history you will find many aristocratic rulers and nobles who acquired their position through birthright, warriors who were the champions of their tribes and nation states, top religious officials appointed or chosen by their own, often nepotistic, friends and relations, and, to a lesser extent, a few people who achieved prominence through ingenuity or business acumen. Because people of lesser social status could not inherit a title and are not usually educated among the children of the elite in a society, they had (and still have) fewer opportunities to practice leadership and must take the paths that are open to them to rise in status by merit. These realities furthered the notion that leadership was an inherent quality, and, for the most part, a masculine trait bestowed at birth.

Mary Parker Follet: Pioneering Feminine Attributes in Leadership

Wouldn't you know it? Eventually, the vision for an ethical, caring, teamwork approach to organizational leadership evolved out of the economic research of a woman born in the era of the second industrial revolution: Mary Parker Follett.

In the early part of the twentieth century, American Mary Parker Follett, a woman whom organizational consultant Warren Bennis called a "pioneer, a swashbuckling advanced soul of management thinking" because of how she applied her talents to studying organizational management and leadership.[4]

In 1898, Follett graduated summa cum laude from Radcliffe University (at the time known as the Society for the Collegiate Instruction of Women) in Cambridge, Massachusetts, the sister school to Harvard, exclusively designated for the education of women. In 1924, she published *Creative Experience*, her third book, which incorporated her ideas about the relationships of leaders and followers in a group process. She moved to England to work and study at Oxford University and subsequently was invited to become a lecturer at the London School of Economics.

Throughout her career, Follett advocated for more effective interactions between managers and workers. She was interested in the personal fulfillment of workers and the creation of a just society. She looked at the art of leadership more holistically than her predecessors, foreshadowing our contemporary approaches, particularly those that balance feminine and masculine leaderships attributes.

Follett is sometimes referred to as the "mother of conflict resolution"[5] because she believed you had to account for the various conflicting needs and desires of different people in the workplace when managing and leading. She identified a leader as someone who sees the whole picture rather than only the individual parts.

In her essay "Power," Follett coined the phrases *power-over* and *power-with* to differentiate coercive power from participative decision-making, showing how *power-with* can be greater than *power-over*. "Do we not see now," she observed, "that while there are many ways of gaining an external, an arbitrary power—through brute strength, through manipulation—genuine power is always that which inheres in the situation?"[6]

With our modern-day, fear-based mindset of separation and the me-me-me point of view expanding to affect the entire world population, Follett's humanistic perspective seems like a much-needed influence. In Follett's book *The New State*, published in 1918 following the global chaos and destruction of World War I, she writes:

> *Within every individual is the power of joining himself fundamentally and vitally to other lives, and out of this vital union comes the creative power. . . .*
>
> *No individual can change the disorder and iniquity of this world. No chaotic mass of men and women can do it. Conscious group creation is to be the social and political force of the future. Our aim must be to live consciously in*

more and more group relations and to make each group a
means of creating. It is the group which will teach us that
we are not puppets of fate.[7]

The Post-World War II Culture of Leadership

In the late 1940s and early 1950s, a series of leadership studies broadened our *then* understanding of the post-war social, economic, and political needs for effective leadership. Let's talk about a few.

One of the most significant researchers, Ralph M. Stogdill, a professor of management science and psychology at Ohio State University, did a survey of the literature and wrote numerous articles offering evidence that persons who are good leaders in one situation won't necessarily be good leaders in other situations.[8] The idea that leadership is a response to the needs of a particular situation has frequently dominated discussions of management ever since.

Theories of **situational leadership** call for leaders to learn different types of responses they might use when confronted by a variety of diverse situations and circumstances. A leader is said to have a situational leadership style when he or she chooses the best course of action based upon the variables of the scenario at hand.

Transactional leadership, also known as *managerial leadership,* pertains to supervision, organization, and group performance. Leaders who utilize this model view the relationship between managers and subordinates as exchanges. In most cases, this means a leader says to a worker, "If you work for me, I will remunerate you financially (both with cash and with benefits such as health insurance, stock options, an expense account, a vehicle, paid vacation days, and so on) for your time and effort."

Primarily a system of rewards and punishments, transactional leadership is still predominantly used in commerce and businesses: When employees are successful and meet given goals, their performance is sometimes rewarded with increases in pay and promotions to higher levels of status and responsibility. When they don't, they are reprimanded, ignored, let go, or demoted.

Rules, procedures, and standards are essential in transactional leadership. Employees usually are not encouraged to be creative or to find new solutions to problems. While research has found that transactional leadership can be effective in situations where problems are simple and clearly defined, it is generally considered unsatisfactory because it prevents both managers and staff from achieving their full potential. Given the disadvantages of the style, no wonder employees today frequently experience significant burnout and depression and, on occasion, prefer remote working.

What generally ends up happening is that individuals (both leaders and followers) working within the transactional leadership model become interested exclusively in the extrinsic rewards they are supposed to get from their work, like prestige or a paycheck. There is a high degree of employee disengagement up and down the organizational ladder. Leaders who have risen through the ranks of this model are generally not interested in nurturing their followers. Employees, sensing they are not appreciated or cared for, default into a self-induced malaise, depression, and lack of initiative.

Transformational leadership occurs when leaders and followers motivate one another to advance to higher levels of morale and motivation. Through the strength of their vision and personality, transformational leaders can inspire their followers to change their expectations, perceptions, and motivations, and work toward common goals.

Bernard Bass, Ph.D., founding director of the Center for Leadership Studies at Binghamton University, characterized transformational leadership as "lifting people into their better selves."[9] This style is not mutually exclusive from any other and it is widely researched because it has shown substantial increases in performance, effectiveness, employee wellbeing, and motivation. These kinds of leaders often become mentors to subordinates whose self-growth and individual development they encourage. They provide meaning, serve as role models, and create learning experiences within a framework of trust.

Autocratic leadership is characterized by the following distinction. If the leader is the most knowledgeable and experienced member of an organization or team, the leader may lead by command, as an authority figure. If members of a work team are equally proficient and experienced, a *democratic leadership* approach might be more applicable to deciding upon a course of action.

What I have personally encountered from time to time in organizations that avow they practice consensus or simple majority decision-making is that the members of the team provide guidance, ideas, and expert opinions to a team leader. These contributions often are ignored in favor of the autocratic, I-am-in-charge individual pursuing a personal agenda. I'm sure many readers could recognize these individuals.

Autocratic leadership is when one individual has control over all decisions, which are typically made based on that person's own judgment with little or no input, even from those who can provide expert guidance and analysis. (Witness the four years of chaos the United States endured between 2016 and 2020 due to an autocratic presidency). What's always so surprising to me is that autocrats don't seem to realize that the teams of experts which they are ignoring clearly perceive how the autocrats behaves. Their lack of self-awareness sabotages and undermines any truly effective leadership they might presume to have. Autocratic leadership will ultimately fail in team-led organizations.

This style of leadership could occasionally be appropriate if the leader has confidential information. Despite the periodic need for a peremptory decision in every type of organization, those who utilize this leadership style tend to be disliked and resented by coworkers more than those who have a more communal leadership style.

We will hear from some modern-day transcendental leaders further into the book, as to how they lead with a communal *serve-the-whole leadership* style.

Psychologically speaking, people like to be heard and to feel that their presence and input matters. Fortunately, current research shows that a democratic, diverse, and inclusive leadership style provides people within an organization a more participatory role leading to greater productivity, more creative problem-solving, and an increased esprit de corps.

An Attitude of Service

The term *servant leadership* was first coined by management researcher Robert Greenleaf, founder of the Robert K. Greenleaf Center for Servant Leadership, in his 1970 essay "The Servant as Leader."[10] Although his conception of the servant as leader came partly out of his experience in working to shape large institutions, in my research I discovered that the pivotal event that generated his axiom of the servant-leader, came about in the 1960s, when he read Hermann Hesse's novella *Journey to the East*.

You may recall that in the story, the narrator, H.H., is a German choirmaster who is invited on an expedition through space and time with a secret sect known as the League. Members of the League include Mozart, Plato, Pythagoras, Puss 'n' Boots, and Don Quixote, among others, both real and fictional. Their journey is a pilgrimage to the "home of the light," where everyone expects to find the *ultimate truth*. A harmonious beginning eventually dissolves into conflict and distrust, with one lone person—a lowly servant named Leo—trying to maintain a cohesive experience.

Eventually, Leo disappears, and in the aftermath, without his gentle presence, one by one each member feels the rest of the group is intolerable, departs the group and gives up their quest.

This brings the pilgrimage to an end without anybody finding either light or truth.

Years later, H.H. has fallen into deep despair and feels called to search for Leo, the humble, compassionate, and gentle servant. After finding Leo, he is asked by Leo to accompany him to a meeting of the League. At the meeting, H.H. discovers that Leo is and always was the president of the League and that the original pilgrimage was a spiritual test. He realizes: "For our goal was not only the East, or rather the East was not only a country and something geographical, but it was the home and youth of the soul, it was everywhere and nowhere, it was the union of all times."[11]

After reading this story, Greenleaf concluded that its central meaning was that a great leader is first experienced as a humble servant to others and that this simple fact is central to the leader's greatness. He believed that sincere leadership emerges from those whose primary motivation is a deep desire to serve others.

Who is a servant-leader? Greenleaf says:

> It begins with the natural feeling that one wants to serve, to serve first. Then conscious choice brings one to aspire to lead. The difference manifests itself in the care taken by the servant, to first make sure that other people's highest-priority needs are being served. The best test is: Do those served grow as persons; do they, while being served, become healthier, wiser, freer, more autonomous, more likely themselves to become servants? And what is the effect on the

least privileged in society? Will they benefit or, at least, not be further deprived?[12]

As we shall explore in a future chapter, service to the whole is one of the three main traits of transcendental leadership. Servant leadership doesn't quite go as far. It is a precursor, however, and alludes to serving the employees and not necessarily the whole.

The Integrated Psychological Model

This modality of leadership endeavors to develop one's presence and psychological self-mastery. This theory gained recognition with a book published in 2011 by executive coach James Scouller, *The Three Levels of Leadership*.[13] He is one of the first to research and write about how successful leaders must work on their inner, personal self-awareness and psychology. To inspire others, a person must have a certain quality of emotional presence and to be genuinely inspiring, create trust, and provide motivation.

In his book, Scouller proposes the ***three levels of leadership theory***, which summarizes what leaders need to address to both provide leadership to others and to psychologically develop themselves. The first two levels include behavioral skills to influence groups and individuals. The third level focuses on the leader's own self-development, personal awareness, and skill set. He asserts that psychological self-mastery is necessary for the development of personal leadership presence, which includes leaders "walking their talk" in terms of their personal values, building trusting relationships, and reevaluating one's limiting beliefs.

From the perspective of traits exemplified by a transcendental leader, Scouller is on the right track.

The Contemporary Vanguard: Conscious Leadership

A conscious leader is someone aware of all aspects of life as an integrated being. Someone who is awake to the interconnectedness of the four pillars of intelligence.

- Emotional intelligence: the capacity to pause, observe and manage our auto-triggered emotions, which then, can influence our responses. In addition, we also have the ability to perceive and impact the same in others
- Physical intelligence: the ability to embody the relationship between the mind and the physical body, in addition to the capacity to feel and exhibit the energies from fields of coherence
- Intellectual intelligence: the aptitude to think strategically, make extensive plans, possess mental acumen, understand complex ideas, and to creatively solve challenging situations
- Spiritual intelligence: the capacity to incorporate realms of higher wisdom, compassion, authenticity and love

A conscious leader leads with awareness of all the stakeholders involved in a situation and with the highest interests of all those involved as well. Conscious leadership encompasses the important attributes of purpose, authenticity, mindfulness, and transparency. It hopes to assist organizations and conscious businesses to think in terms of regenerative sustainability and is mindful of the wellbeing of their employees and the planet. By contrast, unconscious leadership is that which causes harm, indifferently, or even accidentally. Like a factory that leeches pollutants into nearby rivers as its management team remains exclusively focused on generating profits.

Of course, there are a myriad of other leadership theories. As mentioned, I'm only highlighting a few here in order to set the stage of our journey together.

A Pivotal Moment in History

We know that there was an exchange of knowledge and a leap of conscious awareness that occurred during the first known *axial age*, which historians view as lasting from about the eighth to the third century B.C.E. This was a turning point for civilization, a pivotal period in which great thinkers, sages, prophets, and philosophers from different world cultures—most notably from China, India, the Greco-Roman Empire, and Persia—were exploring new and profound philosophical and spiritual ideas and concepts that were similar. Interestingly, not only were these great thinkers emerging from distinct cultures, but they were also worlds apart from each other in actual distance.

What arises for me when I think about this phenomenon is how it represents a field of coherence on a worldwide scale, akin to the concept of a *critical mass*. Like a tuning fork resonating with the strings of a piano, the frequencies of certain ideas were arising in the minds and souls of highly evolved individuals around the world who had the capacity to tune in to a collective field of evolving conscious awareness. Their mutual advancements in remote locations were a potential arising from the unseen unified field.

We are *now* experiencing a new axial age. Perhaps induced by the myriad challenges we face, our collective consciousness today is rapidly evolving to align the heart, mind, body, and soul of leaders and people in general alike. People everywhere are developing a heightened awareness of nature and their place within the environment.

Our extraordinary communication technologies allow more people than ever before to share and exchange ideas and have mutual experiences of revelation, self-realization, contemplative practice, and transcendent awareness.

We are on the threshold of awakening to a new level of consciousness in which all human beings recognize they are one with and through Source. The transcendental leader embodies this realization.

REFLECTION EXERCISE

Take a few minutes to reflect on the following assumptions. Think and feel as to whether you are open to these guiding elements. Which ones might you already embrace? Which ones might you need to further ponder? Which ones would be a stretch for you for you to accept?

- The transcendental leader acknowledges the unity and oneness of the cosmos.

- The transcendental leader accepts that there is loving presence or *force* permeating all things.
- The transcendental leader practices accessing this guiding Source of universal wisdom and presence.
- The transcendental leader implements the universal wisdom received.

II

TRANSCENDENCE AND WISDOM IN LEADERSHIP

*Transcendental leaders believe that there is a
foundational and guiding source of universal wisdom
and intelligence permeating the entire cosmos.*

There are numerous chronicled references to states of transcendence and its effect on the being of leaders throughout known history. In this chapter, I will share a few examples of transcendence from diverse ancient philosophical and wisdom traditions along with the findings of leading-edge contemporary scientific investigations that are discovering that everything is fundamentally interconnected. The essential nature of consciousness and our relationship with the entire universe is often revealed to people in states of transcendence. This information will provide a framework for our conversation and journey into transcendental leadership and its foundational principles.

I define transcendence as an experiential state and as an energetic frequency that arises within us and showcases an awareness that lies above our normal personal perceptions of the world of experience (our subjective reality). As humans, many of us seem to yearn for a more enhanced state of conscious awareness. Almost everyone will experience occasional moments of heightened awareness, times when we realize we exist independently of our individual ego and at the same time sense that we are inextricably and completely connected to the entire cosmos—to everyone and *everything* in it.

This sensation is borne out by evidence from science. As renowned management consultant Margaret J. Wheatley, Ed.D., says: "We know from science that nothing in the universe exists as an isolated or independent entity."[1]

During moments of transcendence, we acquire a seamless ability to envision, feel, and perceive the numinous grace and presence of Source. In these moments, we experience:

- *A peak:* a high state of awareness of our connection to Source.
- *A peek:* the veil of illusory perception drops, and we are able to perceive a new and different conception or image of reality.
- *Being piqued:* We feel a physical and embodied sense of excitement, allure, and curiosity associated with a deep emotional resonance—feeling the presence of wonder, epiphany, and a coherent connection to everything and its Source.

Our ancient ancestors may have more assiduously cultivated these *holy* moments than we do in our noisy, technology-driven civilization. Living more intimately attuned to nature, they would have recognized how we can be momentarily lifted to a state of being that exceeds our intellectual and physical reality. Throughout history, mystics, prophets, sages, seers, and philosophers have taught and nurtured practices to cultivate such states, which, unfortunately, were generally offered only to the elite or to religious acolytes inhabiting remote locations.

I don't want us to get ahead of ourselves here. In a later chapter we will explore various types of practices that are conduits—or *portals,* as I term them—for insight, transformation, and alignment to states of transcendence and connection to Source.

Transcendence complements the process of awakening. Our world's most renowned philosophers, prophets, mystics, thinkers, and spiritual teachers have experienced moments of enlightenment and the realization of connection to Source. They have attempted to share their wisdom and knowledge derived from such experiences to the best of their ability. There are many references to be found in ancient texts and holy scriptures tying transcendence to leadership. What is equally compelling is the modern study of the structure and organization of our cosmos and its relationship to us and all other living organisms.

In my interview with him on transcendental leadership, Joseph Jaworski, author of *Source: The Inner Path of Knowledge Creation,* shared this thought.

When I use the word Source, *there's a dozen or so words that mean the same thing as Source, and that are used interchangeably with it. Some people call it the Implicate Order. That's what my teacher, David Bohm, used. Some call it the Akashic Record, some call it the Field, some call it the Zero Point Field, and I could go on and on. David Bohm also spoke [of it] in later years, and one of his disciples who wrote books with him called it, the field of active information, which is very descriptive, I thought.*[2]

The Gift of Life

Not too many years ago, I went with a good friend to visit Gladwin Planetarium at the Santa Barbara Museum of History, where you sit in a small, dome-shaped theater and can tilt back in a theater-style lounge chair and look up at scenes of stars and planets and constellations moving realistically to simulate the motion of the Heavens. Experiencing the visual imagery is truly awe inspiring. The presentation explains the evolution of our universe, including our solar system and Planet Earth. I was spellbound throughout and came away with a profound realization of something that I rarely think about how our solar system is a miniscule speck in the mindbogglingly enormous infinity of space and our beautiful planetary home is graced with such a myriad of elements that it is capable of sustaining an interconnected system of millions of life forms. OMG, right?!

And here we are, each and every one of us has received the extraordinary gift of a self-aware and conscious life experience on a magnificent blue-green pearl of a planet. Could this be anything less than a miracle, especially given the fact of how your parents' proliferation of egg and sperm created the one and only unique *you?* To me, this does not seem random. When I reflect on the profound mystery of life on Earth, I wonder why I don't get out of bed each morning and fall to my knees in gratitude for this blip of a moment gift of life that I (and you) have been given.

Let us not waste our precious moments of life. Let us love ourselves and each other. Let us freely give and receive. Let us be thoughtful, kind, compassionate, and caring. These qualities provide joy and meaning. Take a moment and truly feel the significance of this and transcendence may embrace your entire being.

Wisdom and Philosophy Found in Transcendence

The word *philosophy* comes from the Greek roots *philo* ("love of") and *sophia* ("wisdom") and means "love of wisdom." We historically attribute this body of rhetorical knowledge to the earliest known western philosophers, the ancient Greeks mentioned in literature, such as Socrates, Plato, Aristotle, and others. Research implies that the promulgation of their ideas aligned with the Axial Age of the Great Transformation—a pivotal time in history when humanity began to ask self-reflective questions, such as "Who am I?" Interestingly, humanity was experiencing this evolution in consciousness in many regions across the globe. A critical mass of cross-cultural connections with philosophical, spiritual, and intellectual thought was occurring throughout the empires of the East, occurring in China, India, Persia, Egypt, and Greece at basically the same time.

TRANSCENDENTAL LEADERSHIP

The works of many early Greek philosophers indicate their interest in exploring self-knowledge, including reflection on the experience of transcendent awareness. For example, in the fourth century B.C.E. Heraclitus of Ephesus wrote his book *On Nature*. It was divided into three sections: cosmology, theology, and politics. In it, he says: "I searched within myself and found my nature."[3]

Although these words may not be exact, he is saying that when he deeply reflected within himself, he found his inner Source (nature). A characteristic of this was his capacity for transcendent connection to the Divine, the whole of nature, and the cosmos. This is the same transcendent experience most of us refer to when we use the terms *awakening* and *realization*. We "awaken" to Source indwelling within us and we "realize" that we are an aspect of Source. The most basic tenet of both self-knowledge and wisdom is the understanding and experiential knowing that we embody Source—or, in other words, the whole of nature, universal wisdom, and the cosmos.

How could Source not be embodied within us?

When we connect to the significance of this understanding and allow it to permeate our awareness, a state of transcendence comes alive in our presence. In this state of transcendence, our frequency becomes more attuned to and aligned with Source.

For many individuals, having this experience is a clarion call for the cultivation of transcendental leadership. We become drawn to lead from a state of transcendence.

However, before we can authentically and transparently lead one another, we first need to lead our personal lives guided by this inner transcendent awareness, because we lead from our state of *being*, not from our state of *doing*. We can learn skills of management, yes, but people only "follow" us because they are attracted to our consciousness and the frequency we generate.

Heraclitus also sagely wrote: "What is wise is one thing: *to know the thought* that directs all things."[4] The one thing—the thought—is Source, that which *directs all things.*

This notion of there being *only one thing* is a recurring theme in the sacred texts of Buddhism, Hinduism, Taoism, and ancient Greek philosophy, and is evidence of the underlying spiritual unity among people of every culture. Every human being is capable of sensing connection with the natural world, universal wisdom, and the cosmos—and—of being awakened to it.

Buddhists tell a story of how, in the Buddha's early ministry, a group of monks came to listen to his words of wisdom. They were so impressed with what he had to say that one of them asked, "Who are you anyway? Are you a god or are you a saint?"

Buddha replied: "I am awake."

In Buddhism, the traditional definition of realization and enlightenment is to be fully present. The moment of transition to full *presence,* the defining characteristic of enlightenment, is *being awakened.*

Heraclitus searched his nature and found a quality of being that is known by different names, such as presence, Source, God, realization, enlightenment, One Mind, and divinity. Buddha's enlightened awakening emerged as a direct response to his human experience of *searching his own inner nature*—through deep, contemplative silence to a process of inner inquiry and surrender. Any individual aspiring to be a transcendental leader is similarly called to deep, personal reflection as one of their primary practices.

Searching our inner nature also requires deep listening. When I search deeply within my own nature I am able to connect with my inner self (found in the silence that exists in the gaps between thoughts and behind sense perceptions) and I also experience a transcendent relationship to Source. The experience of quiet, inner inquiry resonates with me so much that living a conscious and aware life has become my purpose and passion.

I went to a Catholic school growing up where the students went to Mass each morning. This must have been an early, formative exercise in which I learned and gained the capacity to quiet my mind and be reflective and contemplative. Maybe it was only because I'd had a lot of practice that by the time I was attending the University of Washington when the opportunity presented itself to learn Transcendental Meditation (TM) I was all in! I was majoring in psychology in the era when the Beatles introduced their guru, Maharishi Mahesh Yogi, the founder of TM, to the western world.

Here we are, many years later, and the mantra I was given at age twenty is still a predominant practice for me. I've learned other meditation practices and often incorporate them as well. I feel I can intuitively sense Source's guidance more clearly when I keep up my various practices of meditation.

Most people my age who learned TM back in their college days were not of the older, corporate, white-collar variety. That era was, admittedly, the hippie era. We wore bell-bottom jeans, tie-dyed shirts, and long dresses (the girls!), and grew our hair long. I took the required TM course and was given my mantra. I enjoyed the practice right from the get-go—and umpteen years later, I can attest that TM has been a very important and positive tool, contributing immensely to all aspects of my life. It's provided me with glimpses of transcendence and deep peace in times of anxiety and fear. It's helped me be emotionally strong when needed and to find courage in challenging situations.

Just knowing that I had this tool in my toolbox of life skills gave me confidence. I learned I could access fields of creativity with consistency (as do comedian Jerry Seinfeld and musician Paul McCartney, and neither is a one-hit wonder). I receive ideas—more ideas than I know what to do with, in fact.

One of the most important areas of my life that my meditation practice has contributed to is being a mother. Meditation provides you with the kind of patience needed when, for example, in the middle of a difficult night when your child is sick or having an emotional meltdown. It's a kind of patience which gently arises and you don't know where it could have come from because you are so tired. Meditation helps you learn how to engage in authentic, deep listening, the kind that enables your child to feel safe, heard, and seen. It cultivates the capacity to suspend judgement and reaction. It also gives you the courage and vulnerability to say you're sorry when you've reacted without thinking or are wrong. Our children deserve to be raised by the most emotionally healthy and available versions of us we can be.

Bottom line: Our world needs emotionally healthy leaders, and I believe that a regular meditation practice improves our emotional health. Not only can a regular meditation practice contribute to a quieter mind and overall improved sense of wellbeing, it also raises our frequency—tuning us like tuning forks to the tone of realms attributed to states of inner awareness and Source. And, like a tuning fork—aligns with and shifts the frequency of the field around us. It's why we are often energetically compelled to want to be near extraordinary and profound teachers and leaders.

It should be noted that there are many forms of meditation. Different types of practices light up different regions of the brain and trigger recognizable brainwave patterns. Zen meditation, for example, activates the cingulate cortex and the frontal cortex.[5] Each style of meditation helps us achieve a level of consciousness—a different state—characterized by brainwaves of a specific frequency—everything from calm alertness (alpha) to entrancement (theta).[6] It would be wise to do your homework on various techniques before making a choice of a style to adopt for your regular meditation practice.

As mentioned, we will address tools for transcendence in a later chapter that will showcase various portals you can explore in order to discover the paths that resonate uniquely for you and that can open up your access to and alignment with Source.

In the *Tao Te Ching,* an ancient Chinese philosophical treatise attributed to the sixth-century B.C.E. philosopher Lao Tzu, the founding figure of Taoism, he speaks of the Tao as the evolving and ever-flowing stream of consciousness that is Source. In terms of leadership, Lao Tzu tells us when we are aligned with (and awakened to) Source, the right action, the right strategy, the right plan, and the right decision will arise. Having access to this immense wisdom with minimal effort can enhance our ability to lead and is, therefore, a central component *to leading from a state* of transcendent awareness.

The first time I read a translation of *Tao Te Ching* I had an aha moment and realized: *Slow down. Be more patient. Stop and breathe. Allow things to gently resolve. And especially relax into the deep knowing that the appropriate action (or even no-action) would make itself known.*

This was an interesting notion, leading from an attitude of patience, openness, and deep presence! Letting go and letting Source guide me.

Peter Russell, futurist, philosopher, and author of many books, including *Letting Go of Nothing*, in an interview on transcendental leadership shared with me:

> *When I am grounded in my essential being, abiding in the true self, as some would say, my innate wisdom has the opportunity to guide me. This wisdom is universal in that it is available to all. We just have to step back from the thinking mind, which doesn't always have our best interest at heart (much as it would like to think it does). As we drop back towards our true self, our innate wisdom can shine through more freely. My decisions and actions, will be that much freer from the egoic thinking that can often hamper our leadership potential.*[7]

Deep Presence

As regards the world crises of the early twenty-first century, I feel that, in particular, a key element of leadership is deep presence, as this quality of *being* is required of each of us in so many situations these days.

Let's take a cursory look at this fundamental aspect of our existence.

Our capacity for being fully and deeply present is one of the eternal mysteries that can guide us toward a new vision of awakened consciousness and transcendental leadership. When aligned with the presence of Source, the authentic self emerges. Coupled with the frequency of transcendent leadership, it is inherently compelling.

The friend, colleague, or employee next to you may not know why they are inexplicably drawn to you; they only know you have a compelling presence.

Here is a deep realization: knowing that you are unique in all the world and when you align with Source, putting your unique expression in service to Source, you can be a spiritually aligned, consciously aware human being and exceptional leader to others. You actually can't be anything other than that if you express your uniqueness from your alignment to Source.

Rituals, Trance States, and Seeing Within

The story of Demeter and Persephone, where the daughter of the harvest goddess is kidnapped by the ruler of the underworld, is one of the oldest in Greek mythology. The Eleusinian rites were finely tuned to manifest deep presence, spiritual transformation, and illumination for religious initiates and were timed with nature's cycles. To members of the agrarian culture of the Attica region, not far from Athens, they were considered essential to the survival of humanity. Many of the rituals practiced are thought to have been celebrated since the Neolithic era, some 12,000 years ago. The myth of the mother and daughter, a sacred story of separation and reunion, served as a catalyst for planting and harvesting in sync with the seasons. The rites were symbolic of the natural laws of the seasons, birth, growth, death, and regeneration.

Today, as well as in antiquity, preparation for rituals that bring us into a trance state where we can experience our connection with Source often requires emotional, physical, and spiritual purification through cleansing, fasting and detoxing, atonement, silence, and solitude. Before the Eleusinian rites, preparations would have helped participants enter a physical, emotional, and spiritual state of consciousness that allowed them to attain *epopteia*—the state of transcendence necessary for *seeing within*. The rituals took them into the numinous deep mysteries of their inner selves, nature, and the cosmos.

An important element of the Delphic Oracle and the rituals of the early Greek Eleusinian Mysteries was the ingestion of a hallucinogen—whether through inhalation from a cleft in the floor of the temple, as in the case of the Delphic Oracle, or by drinking the psychoactive brew *kykeon,* which was most likely made of some fermented grains, as in the case of the Eleusinian Mysteries.

The rituals of preparation provided an initiate with the ability to experience deep presence, transformation, and psychological states of illumination and transcendence. Many similar rituals were, and still are, utilized by retreat centers, spiritual teachers, religious ceremonies, and people of Indigenous cultures in their ceremonies and spiritual practices to experience a sacred, numinous reality imbedded in presence.

It is no secret as to the contemporary and popular use of the ayahuasca vine originally discovered by tribesmen in the Amazon jungle or the peyote cactus by Native Americans, among other entheogenic brews, teas, and herbs now utilized in ceremonies by people around the world performed with the intention to raise spiritual and conscious awareness.

Another important factor in ancient Eleusis was that the seasonal rituals were facilitated by a priestess or goddess initiate. Known as the Pythia, this woman held court within the cave of the temple. An oracle, she would *channel* wisdom while in a transcendent trance or dreamlike state of consciousness. She would embody divine presence and speak on behalf of the gods and goddesses worshipped by her culture.

The fact that these renowned sacred rites, which are still well known and recognized today, were facilitated by a woman aligned with Source and primarily offered *for* women is important to remember, as leadership traits and characteristics balance both the feminine and the masculine attributes of transcendental leadership.

Greek initiates were said to have experienced transcendence and self-realization, a vision of the beginning and the end, birth, death and rebirth, descent and ascent, and an encounter with the divine presence of Source. Their everyday notions of seeing and perceiving evolved from a state focused on survival to a state of holy divine communion. Experiencing transcendence contributed to spiritual and intellectual evolution throughout the Greek world.

As mentioned, many of these foundational rituals and practices are still utilized in retreat programs, wisdom traditions, and Indigenous groups when they are preparing themselves for deep self-inquiry, transcendent rituals, and spiritual realization.

Transcendental Thought

In the history of philosophy, the notion of deep presence and the experience of the transcendent appear frequently. One of the individual philosophers I personally resonate with is Ralph Waldo Emerson. I was properly reintroduced to Emerson and the American Transcendentalist Movement through my philosophy studies for my master's degree in consciousness. I found Emerson's thinking compelling and fell in love completely. I must thank one of my professors, Richard G. Geldard, Ph.D., a maestro of Greek and Emersonian philosophy, for introducing me to his writings and awakening in me a profound connection to these deep thinkers.

In Emerson's essay "Nature" (1836), he writes:

To go into solitude a man needs to retire as much from his chamber as from society. I am not solitary whilst I read and write, though nobody is with me. But if a man would be alone, let him look at the stars. ...

The stars awaken a certain reverence because though always present, they are always inaccessible; but all natural objects make a kindred impression when the mind is open to their influence. Standing on the bare ground, my head bathed by the blithe air, and uplifted into infinite space, all mean egotism vanishes. I become a transparent eyeball. I am nothing. I see all. The currents of the Universal Being circulate through me; I am part or particle of God.[8]

What Emerson felt in nature was deep presence. In nature, he could sense his connection to Source. Even in reading these few lines, I'm transported—feeling and sensing the awe, reverence, and connection to all. When we learn to access and consistently align with Source, our connection becomes a state of being.

Additionally, in the mid-1800s, Emerson alludes to the qualities that make a great leader when he writes in his essay "The Over-Soul" (1841) *that it is the turning of the eye of one's soul inward* and seeking a relationship with the Divine (Source), what quantum physicist David Bohm called the *Implicate Order*.

> *Let man, then, learn the revelation of all nature and all thought to his heart; this namely: that the Highest dwells with him; that the sources of nature are in his own mind, if the sentiment of duty is there. But if he would know that the great God speaketh, he must 'go into his closet and shut the door' as Jesus said. God will not make himself manifest to cowards. He must greatly listen to himself, withdrawing himself from all the accents of other men's devotion.* [9]

Neuroscientific research continues to reveal the benefits of higher states of consciousness and awareness. Discovering your portals and gateways to Source—and deepening those practices which align our minds, hearts and souls with universal wisdom— brings about states of greater awareness, clarity, wisdom, peace, intuition, and transcendence in our everyday lives too.

Theurgy

Another direct benefit of the portals to transcendence is that they enhance our spiritual awareness or *theurgy*. Emersonian expert, Dr. Geldard describes *theurgy* as an "ancient term meaning the direct intervention of divinity into the individual as a force of energy." [10]

As a leader, having divine force within us provides us with greater compassion, clarity, and wisdom. Spiritual knowledge is something that many people attempt to gain over a lifetime, hoping to eventually reach the greater goal of wisdom. The transcendental leader understands that what makes them wise is their capacity for deep listening which enables them to tap in to the Implicate Order of the cosmos and the presence of Source. To access divine Source requires their willingness to remain open to learning, to receiving, to awakening, and to sharing.

Spiritual Wisdom Traditions and Transcendence

Spiritual presence and transcendence have been recognized by mystics and leaders of the major religious and wisdom traditions since history began to be written. Although each tradition describes this awareness a little bit differently, they all share an understanding of it as a core element of both the individual's journey and the collective's evolutionary journey towards transcendent self-realization and connection to Source. These are variously known as the One Mind (Buddhism), the Great Spirit (Indigenous cultures), Brahman (Hinduism), and the Kingdom of God (mystical Christianity).

For instance, in the Buddhist tradition, quieting the mind is understood to lead to the dissolution of separation between the ego/self and the outer world. Christians associate contemplative prayer with grace and the Holy Spirit of God. In Islam, particularly the mystical sect of Sufism, contemplative prayer with its quieting of the mind is known as *opening the heart.*

The sacred scriptures and texts of the world's predominant religions and wisdom traditions provide instructions to guide us in taking the intellectual and spiritual journeys of the human spirit. The key themes found throughout these texts include loving thy neighbor as thyself; self-awareness; and a movement from an outward-projected divinity to the realization that the "kingdom" of divinity is within. In addition, these sacred texts inspire positive social action that contributes to the wellbeing and service to all.

It should be mentioned that although each of the major traditions originated in a different region of the world, within a unique culture, and at a distinct time in history, all tap into and share the *same underground river of wisdom* as the others. The deep wisdom that underlies various teachings, albeit expressed in different languages, rituals, and practices, is essentially the same: Humanity and the world at large are divine and connected. We are brothers and sisters made out of the same stuff: starlight, stardust, and the One Mind I call Source.

A common term for the eternal wisdom that transcends epoch and culture is *perennial philosophy.* I'm sure you have all heard the phrase. In essence, it's the notion of philosophical insight that is universally sanctioned and independent of culture and historical era. Perennial philosophy is a perspective that views the world's individual religions and traditions of wisdom as having a shared universal truth—and a single divine foundation. It is expressed in diverse ways in individual cultures, scriptures, and history because local religions were cultivated to fit with the social, political, cultural, and emotional needs of a time and people.

Although the term was coined in the 1500s by Renaissance humanist August Steuco, the book *The Perennial Philosophy* by the British writer Aldous Huxley, made it famous in 1945.

In the Introduction, Huxley describes perennial philosophy as:

The metaphysic that recognizes a divine Reality substantial to the world of things and lives and minds; the psychology that finds in the soul something similar to, or even identical with, divine Reality; the ethic that places mans' final end in the knowledge of the immanent and transcendent Ground of all Being; the thing is immemorial and universal. Rudiments of the perennial philosophy may be found among the traditional lore of primitive peoples in every region of the world, and in its fully developed forms it has a place in every one of the higher religions.[11]

Perennial philosophy has become its own genre: *perennialism.* Huxley did a comprehensive and thorough analysis of quotes, scriptures, and texts of known saints, mystics, sages, and shamans of all known theologies and religions, including Hinduism, Buddhism, Taoism, Islam, Judaism, and Christianity. He chose a smorgasbord of quotations and passages from, for example, Rumi, St. John of the Cross, Buddha, Meister Eckhart, the Upanishads, and the Bhagavad Gita to provide a perspective and global synthesis that underscores the idea that all the wisdom traditions of the world share a common metaphysical truth.

He writes:

The nature of this one Reality is such that it cannot be directly and immediately apprehended except by those that have chosen to fulfill certain conditions, making themselves loving, pure in heart, and poor in sprit.[12]

To be "poor in spirit" means having humility. Huxley understood that the path to relationship with the one Reality

(Source) is found through embodying the qualities and attributes of a transcendental leader: loving, compassionate, transparent, and humble.

Now, let's explore the major traditions of spiritual wisdom in the world by looking at excerpts from their scriptures and teachings that showcase their understanding of the nature of transcendence and its interrelationship with leadership and connection to Source. For the sake of brevity in this book, I'm only sharing a few examples, as there are numerous way showers to be found in all the sacred texts.

Transcendence in the Ancient Teachings of Hinduism

What practices would benefit contemporary leaders to borrow and adapt from an ancient theology? Well, the fundamental teachings of the Hindu scriptures provide instructions for leading a life aligned with illumined leadership—so that's a good place to investigate. *The Bhagavad Gita ("The Song of God")* is one of the most meaningful spiritual texts on dharma (the right course of action) known to humankind. In it, the divine being of Krishna, an avatar, spiritual master, and teacher appearing in human form, serves as the charioteer for Prince Arjuna, leader of a tribe (in ancient India) during a battle against his own brethren from a neighboring area. Arjuna is unaware that his servant is a god incarnate—a god manifesting as a spiritually illumined human being.

This epic story is a parable that includes dialogues on philosophy, spirituality, *transcendental leadership,* and cosmic law transpiring on a battlefield some 5,000 years ago. Many people consider its contents as relevant today as when it was written. *The Gita,* as it is colloquially known, showcases the causes of humanity's problems to be inherently embedded with human nature, which is limited by egoistic attachments. As Krishna explains these causes, he offers Arjuna answers that lead to detachment, which informs his illumined dharma of right action.

The timeless message of *The Gita* does not refer only to one historical battle. In fact, it is a metaphor for the perennial conflicts we face in life between right and wrong, attachment and detachment, ignorance and knowledge, the spiritual and the material, and the divine and the mundane. Krishna teaches Arjuna that leading a spiritual life does not require renunciation of work and action, but rather that we should respect the responsibilities of our daily lives while maintaining a higher consciousness.

Think of Arjuna as an unenlightened leader, diligently working hard, stressed and unhappy in his job. After illumination, he recognizes his innate divinity and becomes a transcendental leader with Source manifesting through him.

These days, even more so than in many historical periods, humanity is being called to arise out of our suffering and ignorance, and to ascend into our divine nature and consciousness. This is the call of the transcendental leader. Through a philosophy of divine works, the awakened individual, claiming and imbued with their divine nature, attributes their actions to guidance from Source.

Along these same lines, in *The Life Divine,* twentieth-century Indian philosopher Sri Aurobindo writes:

The liberated man is not afraid of action, he is a large and universal doer of all works, krstsna-karma-krt; not as others do them in subjection to Nature, but poised in the silent calm of the soul, tranquilly in Yoga with the Divine. To do all in this liberating knowledge, without the personal egoism of the doer, is the first sign of the divine worker.[13]

If *The Gita* is to be given credence, then leaders should strive for freedom from their attachment to a personally desired outcome. They should aim to work as instruments of Source and universal wisdom. The egocentric person leads from his personal attachments, whereas the transcendently aligned person leads for the welfare of the world. But with the recognition that it is Source, whose presence is within us, who guides us.

Integral to Hinduism is the tradition of yoga ("yoking to" or "being in union" with the Divine). Yoga has four paths: *bhakti yoga* (the path of love and devotion), *jnana yoga* (the path of knowledge), *karma yoga* (of the path of service), and *raja yoga* (the path of meditation). Any of these, with a regular practice, together or separately, can unlatch the doors to transcendent experience.

In Chapter 4, I will go into more depth about the yoga system originating from *The Yoga Sutras of Patanjali.* The eight practices he outlined in his scrolls, known as the true yoga, are ancient and time-honored practices that can help a leader experience alignment with states of transcendent awareness and Source.

Transcendence in the Story of the Buddha's Awakening

The Four Noble Truths of Buddhism came to Siddhartha Gautama on the night he sat in deep meditation beneath a Bodhi tree by a river, having sworn to himself that he would not move from that spot until he attained complete enlightenment. He had searched and journeyed for many years in an attempt to gain transcendent enlightenment. While deeply immersed in his meditation, he sifted through layers of deepening awareness.

Siddhartha eventually merged with Source and became the Buddha. At this moment of enlightened awareness, he realized the connection and relationship between all things. He understood that humanity's ignorance was central to our suffering. The truth he realized at that moment was that life inevitably includes suffering and our innate desire to fill the void of separateness is the root cause of it.

Buddha also realized that we could stop suffering by following the Eightfold Path, or Middle Way. This involves following a path midway between the excesses of self-indulgence and the restrictions of self-renunciation. It is through adherence to "right" practices that our ignorance of the illusion of separateness and our attachment to material things gradually dissipate and suffering diminishes.

The practices of the Eightfold Path are:
- Right thinking,
- Right livelihood,

- Right speaking,
- Right intentions,
- Right behavior,
- Right mindfulness,
- Right effort, and
- Right focus.

Whether knowledgeable about the Eightfold Path or not, when leaders embody the precepts of "right living," the individual has stepped onto the path of transcendental leadership.

Transcendence in Islam

In her book *Islam: A Short History,* author and scholar Karen Armstrong writes:

> *Every single human being is a unique and unrepeatable revelation of one of God's hidden attributes, and the only God we will ever know is the Divine Name inscribed in our inmost self.*[14]

Like Buddhism, Islam has core practices called the Five Pillars of the faith. The repetition of these practices provides devotees a way of remembering deep truths about their commitment to God (Source) and their fellow human. Let's consider how they relate to a leader's evolving consciousness.

The first pillar is *shahadah:* bearing witness to your faith, an acknowledgment of God, the Source.

The second pillar is *salat:* praying several times a day in a ritual manner. This is considered the anchor of the religion. Mohammed reportedly taught, "Pray as I pray."

A powerful way to connect with Source is praying, a form of contemplation, devotion, and communication found in all the major spiritual and wisdom traditions. In Christianity, for instance, in the biblical book of Luke 22:19, which recounts the event known as the Last Supper, Jesus says, "Do this in remembrance of me." The ritual celebration of the Mass is modern Christians' equivalent.

Without comparing interpretations of *The Bible* or *The Quran* it is my sense that both of these great messengers of God, Jesus and Mohammed, were sharing a manner of prayer that incorporates ways of aligning to transcendent states and becoming closer to Source.

The Islamic salat postures and gestures, which include kneeling and bowing on a prayer rug, bring to mind the *asanas* of yoga. The ancient yogis discovered that these postures energetically and spiritually aligned their body, mind, and spiritual attunement by opening up channels in the body known as chakras, meridians, and pathways of love, wisdom, and enlightenment.

Muslims find that the social component of praying in a community can provide the amplitude to shift the frequencies and energies of the physical world as well as transform the inner self.

I believe that salat represents a form of bhakti, or devotion in action. In yoga, as was mentioned, bhakti is understood to be one of the four paths to achieving spiritual enlightenment. The social element of group or congregational prayer also creates a collective cultural consciousness that is shared and supported within the context of the whole community.

Regarding the daily frequency of performing the salat, aligned with the cycles of the day (an elemental connection), I propose the following: We are on the scientific frontiers of understanding the brain and the neural pathways of cognitive attention. The more often we pray, contemplate, or meditate on our connection to Source, the more frequently we attune with and can merge with Source and experience transcendence.

Praying and meditative contemplation afford us numinous moments of presence that Mohammed referred to when he said, "Wherever you turn, there is the face of God," and when Jesus said, "The kingdom of God is within," and when the Buddha stated, "The wise are indeed nirvana bound."[15] Each of these spiritual masters sought to teach us that prayer, devotion, and contemplation are portals and gateways to experience Source— everywhere and at any moment.

The more often rituals, or even brief moments of quiet and reflective awareness, prayer, and meditation are practiced, the more the neural pathways of these experiences are exercised and reinforced. New pathways and new default openings of perception become stronger and more likely to occur again and again instead of rarely or only occasionally.

The brain is made up of cells called *neurons*. These cells have nerve endings that release chemical and electrical signals so the cells can communicate with each other. As cells link together from habitual firing of signals, they form chains or networks. Thus, this kind of communication builds new pathways in the brain. At least partly, this is how the brain functions.

When we initially learn something new, the pathway is relatively weak. The more frequently we engage in thinking a particular train of thought, practice the same type of movement, or even feel a similar feeling, the stronger, more durable, and anchored the neuro-pathway associated with that thought, feeling, or movement becomes. Repetition leads to the formation of a more automatic and habitual way of thinking, feeling, perceiving, and experiencing. If this same pathway is used sufficiently, it becomes a *new* default mode of functioning.

As mentioned, in Chapter 4, we will delve into meditation, contemplation, and various other practices that I call *portals* for leaders to explore and examine in order to build and strengthen the pathways in their brains and consciousness that enable them to access both transcendent awareness and their innate inner guidance aligned with Source.

The third pillar of Islam is *sawm*, or fasting, which fundamentally is a way to practice patience. Fasting provides space for self-examination and learning the capacity of self-discipline. It provides the transcendental leader with an important lesson-gift: the gift of *slowing down* and the *capacity to suspend triggered reactions*. Sawn is done during the month of Ramadan in the spring.

Ramadan fasting is usually considered to be the most personal and spiritual of all the pillars because sawn is the one ritual that is, in a sense, *private*. It is only between the individual and Source. (In the Islamic tradition, the name for God is Allah). Allah alone knows whether we have kept to our fast or have taken a sip of water or a small bite to eat. Ramadan is a time of self-examination, discovering the boundaries of our commitments, and our strength for self-discipline.

Research on perception shows that the more stimulation we receive, the less we perceive. To become more receptive to the unseen realms, we need to slow down and become quiet and still. Fasting can help to bring about the thinning of the veil between Heaven and Earth and provide peek/peak/pique holy moments when we feel a sense of numinous, transcendent merging with Source.

The fourth pillar of support is the *zakat*, meaning "purity." It involves symbolic gestures of charity that enable us to purify our wealth. According to Islam, this is a fundamental law: *We are not to treat our own wellbeing as more important than the wellbeing of others.* It is philosophically considered wrong to build private wealth and good to share and create a society where the vulnerable are provided for and treated with respect. Social justice is a fundamental virtue of the Muslim community.

I concur with this belief. It is a fundamental and moral imperative that we should care for one another. I'm saddened by the fear and greed I see in the world. There is a dominant sentiment in our cultural consciousness of "not enough" and separation—so much so, in fact, that many people are afraid to share, be of service, and take care of others compassionately.

To Muslims, participating in acts of social welfare is a sacrament. According to Islam, it is most important to live the life God wants us to live—a life of service to one another.

The Islamic principle of zakat is akin to the yogic principle of *karma*. It is also a precept to which awakened transcendental leaders adhere. The yogic path of karma refers to being of service (doing *seva*). The Islamic principle of zakat (charity) is also service and the care of others.

The final pillar of Islam is *hajj*, making a pilgrimage to the birthplace of the prophet Mohammed. The religious duty is a once-in-a-lifetime journey to the Kaaba ("Cube"), a building at the center of the Great Mosque of Mecca, a city in Saudi Arabia, to do specific rituals there. The pilgrimage is an annual event (although only required once in a lifetime) considered a divine journey and a demonstration of the solidarity of people sharing the Islamic faith.

During the Hajj, everyone wears simple white garments to symbolize equality and purity—showing no outer means of wealth or status. It is celebrated during the last month of the Islamic year in the summer by millions of people praying together, eating together, and commemorating historical events and celebrating the glory of God together.

Transcendence in the Teachings of Jesus, Mystical Christian Saints, and Sacred Places

I used to think that going to sacred places of accrued devotion and reverence was an important aspect of my spiritual journey. However, I now feel that the sacred can be experienced anywhere. Nevertheless, certain spaces hold strong energies that can contribute to the feelings of reverence, sanctuary, and holiness people feel when they are there, especially collectively. Sacro Monte di Orta in Orta San Giulio, Italy, comes to mind as I spent many soulful hours absorbing the magical and mystical energy of this holy site while living in the area. Overlooking the picturesque Lago d'Orta, this is a sacred enclave of twenty small, separate chaplets, each one honoring and depicting twenty significant moments in the life of Saint Francis of Assisi. It is a United Nations Educational, Scientific, and Cultural Organization (UNESCO) World Heritage Site.

It is well known that certain geographical locations on the planet vibrate at different frequencies known to be both healing and/or spiritually uplifting. For example, most of us are familiar with the Holy City of Jerusalem, Stonehenge in Britain, Mount Sinai in Egypt, the Mahabodhi Tree in India, and the region around the geographical landmarks of Uluru and Kata Tjuta in the western desert of Australia. Some of these holy sites are shrines and temples, some are ancient architectural sites, and some are vortices, known for the special frequencies that emanate from the land.

I've been fortunate to explore and immerse myself in quite a few of these sacred places. An adventurer of the spirit, you could say. In summer 2019, I was invited to attend a special pilgrimage to Chartres Cathedral in France, outside Paris. A friend, Jim Garrison, Ph.D., founder and CEO of Ubiquity University, invited me to attend an annual Ubiquity University retreat on the subject of Mary Magdalene and the Black Madonna. This was held in August during the feast days of the Assumption, a day and time of each year when Catholics honor Mary, the mother of Jesus, and celebrate her assumption into Heaven. Our retreat leaders included luminary spiritual teachers, such as Jim, Andrew Harvey, Peggy Rubin, and Anne Baring, plus the magical musician Ruth Cunningham, sacred space cultivator extraordinaire Calen Rayne, and the lovely sacred dancer Banafsheh Sayyed.

Chartres Cathedral has an extraordinary history attributed to its centuries-old mystical energy. It's been documented that Druids and Celtic priests and priestesses held holy rituals on the hill where the cathedral was built. It was considered to be the most important Druid sanctuary of Gaul due to the powerful energy of the land. Underneath the current Cathedral are ancient and holy caves and a watering well, which has long been considered to contain magical, healing waters. Our mystical visits to these venerable caverns and grottos were ethereal. History tells us that the first church was erected there in 350 C.E. Adding to the nuance of its powerful and sacred presence, the Cathedral is located on a ley line linking it with other sacred landmarks, such as Stonehenge, Glastonbury, and the Pyramids of Egypt.

There is evidence that the early residents of the region held sacred rituals and worshipped the Earth goddess on this hill, symbolic of the Divine Feminine, which eventually came to be symbolized by depictions in art of the Black Madonna. When the Catholic Church took possession of the church on the hill around the fourth century, the new cathedral was dedicated to Mary.

Chartres Cathedral has been designated a United Nations Educational, Scientific, and Cultural Organization (UNESCO) World Heritage Site because it is one of the most sacred spaces on our planet. The energy of this sacred site is palpable.

During the retreat, I immersed myself physically, emotionally, and spiritually in a profound and sacred relationship to divine cosmic energy. My most precious moments included quiet time in the subterranean crypt and caves under the Cathedral, early morning private time in the Cathedral before it opened to the public, witnessing the dawning light of sunrise create luminous, crepuscular rays that streamed into the nave through the Cathedral's magnificent stained-glass windows, walking the labyrinth lit with hundreds of tiny votive candles, and watching our brilliant sacred dancer whirling within the vortex of the labyrinth in the candlelight. Evenings, the cathedral and other buildings in the village are lit-up with the renowned light show *Chartres en Lumiere.* Magical. Enchanting. Illuminating.

Over the course of a few days, I was brought to my knees both symbolically, in awe, and literally, when I tripped on the cobblestone walkways and had a terrible fall. This last experience of "being brought to my knees," was both a clear message of embracing humility and to be more present.

For the individual who desires to lead from transcendence, retreats, pilgrimages, vision quests in nature, and time spent in silence and solitude, either alone or with a small group, can bring about transformation, inner epiphanies, Source-inspired creativity, and spiritual messages that come through them. Find a sanctuary of peace and take the time to reconnect with yourself and others in love, contemplation, and deep learning. Immersing yourself in the energy of a sacred place where thousands of people have come to meditate, pray, and perform spiritual ceremonies for thousands of years is inspirational and may provide you with transcendent experiences.

The biblical references to the word *Christ,* in Greek meaning "Anointed One," is a reference to the inherent divine consciousness within all human beings. In this respect, it can be said that Krishna and Buddha, like Jesus, were Christs because they all realized they were a manifestation of the divine godhead in humanity known as *Christ consciousness.*

The Gospel of Mark, which many scholars view as the oldest and most historically accurate gospel in the New Testament of *The Bible,* is important to those who would interpret Jesus' life and the development of his messianic Christ consciousness.

The historical Jesus was a prophet of an oppressed people, a peasant artisan—a carpenter—who taught people they should express love and compassion for others. He saw humanity through eyes immersed in the Divine (Source) and wanted to share the choice of perceiving life with the knowledge of the Divine dwelling within. He taught that this was the location of the kingdom of God, not the sky/Heavens or material comforts. You are likely familiar with the words Jesus said: "The kingdom of God is within you" (Luke 17:21).

Christ consciousness is the mystical relationship with divinity that cannot be adequately described through intellectual or academic parlance. Jesus as Christ and as a man had an intimate relationship with Source and advocated that all human beings—innately—are aspects of the Divine. As is the entire cosmos.

How can it not be?

Religious institutions may formulate, define, structure, and dogmatize the principles of Christianity, but in my opinion, as demonstrated by the human life of Jesus, his contemplative insight of the indwelling of Source within himself and (this really cannot be stressed enough) *all* people and the cosmos was personal, living, spontaneous, and purely spiritual. His personal faith was not the faith of a tradition or an intellectual belief; it was a sublime, transcendent relationship.

Although our records of his life are meager, we know from the few written gospels that survived over two millennia that he demonstrated a profound conviction that securely held him in a place of deep knowing and self-realization—in love, wisdom, and service to the whole.

The profound message of his extraordinary spiritual life was his consciousness of the presence of Source/God within himself, each other, and all of creation. And his greatest teaching was that this presence, wisdom, spiritual realization, and awareness is alive and all around us in the collective field of Source coherence and frequency.

I like to believe that Jesus' sense of having a relationship with the Divine was so absolute that it provided for him the joy and confidence of complete surrender. Jesus did not so much teach his disciples to believe *in* him as to believe *with* him in the reality of the love, presence, and compassion of Source/God. He wanted to share his knowledge. He challenged his disciples to believe in *what* he believed and also to believe *as* he believed. This may be the symbolic significance of Jesus' primary request: "Follow me."

To follow a Christian life means to share a spiritual relationship and connection to Source—and to enter into the spirit of living a life of loving selfless service, another of Jesus' primary messages. In Matthew 22:39, he says: "Love thy neighbor as thyself."

In the context of transcendental leadership, what would loving our neighbors look like in our businesses, institutions, and governments today? How might Jesus or any of these great spiritual masters lead us through the crisis of a global pandemic, political upheaval, or climate change?

Science, Consciousness, and Indra's Net
Leadership, Interconnectivity, and the Implicate Order

For many years, I was a Community Group Leader in Santa Barbara, California, for the esteemed Institute of Noetic Sciences. I would often share this story on leadership, interconnectivity, and the Implicate Order with participants.

Science is leading us to the understanding that we are not separate beings but a community of life. We are connected to each other, the Earth, the stars, and the entire cosmos. There is no narrative more beautifully told than by NASA astronaut

Captain Edgar Mitchell, recollecting his travels back to Earth after having walked for nine hours on the Moon.

Claudia Welss, board chair of the Institute of Noetic Sciences, which Mitchell founded, graciously provided her insights on how Mitchell was impacted by his space adventure.

A very influential example of expanded perception comes from the founder of IONS, Apollo 14 lunar module pilot and sixth man to walk on the moon, Captain Edgar Mitchell, who had an epiphany in space that came to be known the world over as the "Overview Effect." On his way back from his mission, he transitioned from moonwalker to cosmic sightseer, and while gazing at Earth from the lens of space, he suddenly experienced the universe not as a collection of separate objects, but as a loving, intelligent, coherent whole that included himself. This experience was accompanied by a powerful cocktail of awe, humility, and ecstasy, and he would later describe it as a samadhi *experience—an ancient Sanskrit word meaning an intense and heightened state of consciousness characterized by a feeling of oneness with the universe. Captain Mitchell had an embodied experience that "we're all stardust," and as* such *we're not just in the Universe, the Universe is in us. While our outer physical bodies belong to space and time, our inner cosmic nature extends our connections beyond our normal conceptions of space and time.*

Captain Ed Mitchell's epiphany showed him that Agape love, or unconditional love, is the organizing principle of the entire cosmos. Science is demonstrating that unconditional love is an organizing principle in our bodies; how far are we from demonstrating that it's also an organizing principle in our world? I'm not waiting for that scientific proof to discover if unconditional love is an organizing principle in transcendental leadership. I'm already running the experiment, and I encourage you to, too. "[16]

The shift in corporations toward participatory or democratic leadership and management today may be rooted in our changing perspectives of the organizing principles of the universe. Leadership consultant Margaret Wheatley, in *Leadership and the New Science*, writes:

One of the guiding principles of scientific inquiry is that at all levels nature seems to resemble itself. For me, the parsimony of nature's laws is further argument that we need to take science seriously. If nature uses certain principles to create her infinite diversity, it is highly probable that those principles apply to human organizations. There is no reason to think that we are the exception.[17]

What is this new view of the cosmos that is shifting our behavior from the hierarchical model of leadership to a democratic relational team leadership? As Seattle University professor of leadership emeritus John Jacob Gardiner writes:

The essential nature of matter according to the particle-wave metaphor is the essence of living things: the interconnectedness, unified field and web of relationship.[18]

Perhaps unknowingly, Gardiner is conjointly referring to a Buddhist and Vedic teaching known as Indra's Net. This is a metaphor illustrating the interconnected and interdependent cosmic structure of reality, the interbeing of all things, and the intercausality principle of *dependent origination.*

Dependent origination is a core teaching of Buddhism, affirming that everything is interconnected; each thing and moment is a result generated by a multiplicity of originating moments.

In Vedic scriptures from Buddha's time, we learn that Indra was considered to be the ruler of all gods. In *Hua-Yen Buddhism*, Francis H. Cook writes:

Thus, each individual is, at once, the cause for the whole and is caused by the whole and what is called existence is a vast body made up of an infinity of individuals all sustaining each other and defining each other. The cosmos is, in short, a self-creating, self-maintaining, and self-defining organism.[19]

In other words, each of us contains the structure of the cosmos—and every element of the cosmos contains each of us.

Organizational theorists are learning the same thing. Living systems, including organizations, are not assemblages of their parts and people, but are constantly growing and in the process of evolving and becoming. Each *part* is an element in an inseparable web of connection and relationship that functions holo-graphically. This includes systems from the smallest particle to the entire cosmos.

Diane Marie Williams, founder of the Source of Synergy and member of the Evolutionary Leaders Circle, shares:

Transcendental leadership is about knowing from the depth of ones being that we are all part of a field where we are connected to all that is, all that was and all that ever will be. Acknowledging, communicating with, trusting and expressing gratitude for this field and the "nonlocal coworkers" that permeate it, has informed every aspect of my leadership.

In 2006, while meditating, I heard two words, Source and Synergy. Instantaneously, I was intuitively completely clear from a place of deep knowing—that a nonprofit organization was about to be born. One that would tap into the Source and create opportunities for Synergy from this place.

The Source of Synergy Foundation was birthed through trusting the clear direction that came from this holographic universal field, and during our fourteen years, we have warmly welcomed the vast intelligences in various realms of existence to partner with us.[20]

If the world is a holographic living system, then individual actions magnify throughout the systems and networks of the world. The networks then determine the usage of what is magnified, then envelops and shapes the priorities and agendas of worldwide systems. These systems include businesses, governments, institutions, and social realities.

Unfortunately, at this point in time, we live in a culture of materialism, greed, and individualism. We are bombarded by messages from the news media and government leaders interested in securing their power and creating divisiveness, propagating feelings of separateness, fear, and competition. Deeply rooted in our culture is a survival-of-the-fittest mindset. But because the world is holographic, we can use transcendence as each individual's part of the culture to alter the culture. As parts of a living system, everyone has the ability to shift the system.

When I asked Jude Currivan, Ph.D., a renowned cosmologist, planetary healer, and author of the *Cosmic Hologram,* among other works, to share her thoughts and insights into the notion of transcendental leadership, she wrote:

> *In the main, our beliefs drive our behaviors and the stories we tell are generally the ones we live by. Our collective story has reflected a hitherto mainstream scientific perspective enacted through our secular social structures, including our education systems and our financial and economic organizations. Its worldview has been one of materialistic separation and its perspective of an inherently meaningless and randomly evolved universe has determined mechanistic and reductionist approaches that are no longer unsustainable and have become existentially dangerous.*

Now though, leading-edge research at all scales of existence and across numerous fields of scientific investigation is discovering that such a fragmented viewpoint is fundamentally wrong. Instead, more and more discoveries are revealing the nature of reality as being fundamentally interconnected. Even more radical, that our entire universe exists and evolves as a unified reality, with its appearance of space-time and energy-matter emerging from deeper nonphysical realms of causation. And vitally, that mind and consciousness aren't something we have, but rather what we and the whole world are.

The consensus of these findings is describing a universe where everything in existence has intrinsic meaning and worth; a universe that embodies an innate evolutionary impulse and a universe where we are its microcosmic cocreators. This scientifically based whole-world view converges and integrates with universal spiritual traditions and Indigenous wisdom teachings. In doing so, like them, it can't be just understood, but invites and empowers its holism to be experienced and embodied as a lived and loving awareness.[21]

Science is progressing at warp speed and the new information about our universe is trickling into mainstream awareness and affecting how we make decisions in our everyday lives.

Any leader, any person, who understands that the structure of the cosmos and universe is holographically reflected in our structure will experience a "download" and deep sacred inner connection to all. Relationships, decisions, and governing from a connection aligned with Source are hallmarks of transcendental leadership. Leading in truth, compassion, transparency, and love for the whole is the clarion call at this time of awakening.

Amid the chaos and crisis of the years 2020 and beyond, we cannot continue to lead organizations, governments, businesses, and institutions from the mindset that we are separate. Science and the experience of transcendence are telling us that we are connected. And not only are we connected through links between us as individuals, we are also a connected whole. It is time that leaders stop making decisions from a mindset and worldview based on fear and materialistic creed. We must serve the all.

REFLECTION EXERCISE

Take a few moments to consider the following questions.
- What do you think might be the wisdom of nature and the cosmos?
- How have inspired writings of philosophy or sacred scriptures resonated with you?
- What might be your view of expanded human potentials?
- Have you ever had a transcendent experience—and what was it like for you?

III

TRAITS OF
TRANSCENDENTAL
LEADERS

*Namaste. I honor the place in you in which the entire
universe dwells. I honor the place in you that is of truth, of
light, of peace. When you are in that place in you, and I
am in that place in me, we are one.*

In Chapter 1, we explored various models of leadership theory
and why they were predominant at specific times in history. We
talked about the great man theory attributing leadership abilities
"genetically," by breeding, to certain tribes, kings, dynasties, and
aristocratic families. Leadership of the clan or kingdom was
almost always handed down to the oldest son through the
bloodline.

We also took a brief look at situational leadership theory,
transactional leadership theory—which is still prevalent—the
theory of the servant leader, and our trend *du jour,* the theory of
conscious leadership. Common sense suggests that leaders being
consciously aware of the consequences of their actions on the
marketplace, on the people they lead, and those they serve is

beneficial, which means adhering to principles of mindfulness is a step in the right direction. Awareness in this context is not necessarily awareness from a spiritual perspective, but an expression of thoughtfulness about leadership capacities, responsibilities, communications skills, relationships, and the long-term consequences of decisions.

The popularity of this theory speaks to a certain culture of evolving leaders. Leaders who are purpose-driven and think sustainably provide trainings to their employees, teams, and colleagues on emotional intelligence, along with workshops, seminars, and retreats on team-building and sustaining quality relationships. That sounds good, right?

At the Mandali Retreat Center in Italy, where I was consulting until the covid pandemic lockdown, I was happy and excited to create and develop an ongoing program on conscious leadership with Peter Matthies, founder and CEO of the Conscious Business Institute. We had many exciting dialogues about how thoughtful, introspective practices are only recently being acknowledged, addressed, and encouraged within organizations, especially in businesses and governance.

As you can perhaps imagine, the term *transcendental* would freak out most leaders in the business world who are still operating from the collective mindset of the primacy of money and a focus on their return on investment (ROI). What might be deemed a spiritual component to leadership training would definitely sound too woo-woo to them, so this concept isn't yet taken seriously. One day soon, when they understand its advantages, I hope they will reconsider their viewpoint.

The main challenge today is that our global mindset continues suffering from the side effects of one of the main business and economic principles that were introduced in the 1970s and was popularized in the 1980s and 1990s when it became the standard in corporate thinking. This is the notion of *shareholder supremacy*. How well the stock market did during the covid pandemic and its aftermath is evidence of this. The financial elite were making millions even as the people on Main Street were slipping below the poverty line after losing their jobs and falling behind on their mortgages and rent.

The shareholder supremacy mindset is outmoded. It doesn't serve the greater whole, or the needs of our planet. How have we allowed the almighty advertising dollar to take precedence over our innate sense of honesty, human caring, and truth?

It is all too clear that every populace in the world needs to be guided by strong, honest, compassionate, and *awakened* leaders. It is at this juncture of chaos and opportunity that, perhaps, we can spread the new narrative of transcendental leadership.

It should be mentioned, of course, that a number of CEOs, appointed by boards of directors of corporations, and some elected leaders are beginning to see the benefits of a more conscious and aware approach to leading their organizations and governments. But the number remains too few to be significant at this point.

I believe that if we seek greater wisdom humbly and remain curious about ourselves, others (including our animal friends), and the physical world then we can access, acquiesce to, and align with the enormous universal wisdom naturally imbued within each of us.

We are made of the God stuff of the cosmos. And when we are aligned with the deep knowledge within us, it is showcased as emerging traits of the transcendental leader. Each of us—all people everywhere—has this numinous essence within us.

Due to the obvious breakdown of moral, ethical, compassionate, and thoughtful leadership in so many of the countries of the world, now is clearly a moment in time for us to promote a more conscious, spiritual approach. It is so evident that we need leaders endowed and aligned with the attributes that we will discuss here. Now is the time for transformational change in the world.

One caveat, which is mentioned in the Introduction: Traits of a competent leader include so-called hard skills, such as budgeting and forecasting, managing operations, time management; delegation and supervision, and so on, as well as so-called soft skills, such as loyalty, emotional intelligence, self-discipline, the capacity to suspend judgement, relationship building, and so on. I like to think of the latter as *deep skills.*

Following research and inner reflection, it felt strange at first to discover that—truly—there is only *one* overarching trait that all transcendental leaders seek to embody, and that primary trait is the curiosity to understand the true nature of reality and the universe.

For the most part, humanity has no idea what the *true* nature of the universe is. Nonetheless, we inherently strive to understand the meaning of life: Who are we? Why are we here?

These are age-old perennial questions. I think it's an evolving mystery, one perhaps not even possible to be completely understood by us at this moment in time.

For as long as I can remember, even as a child, I've thought about these sorts of philosophical questions. Even though I was raised in a large family, as the only girl among five brothers I had quite a bit of alone time. Perhaps, it was my nature to be a bit of a loner/thinker. This tendency, combined with the catechism/curriculum of the old-fashioned Catholic school I attended, got me *wondering* about the nature of life and our place in it.

When reflecting upon the true nature of reality and the universe, I also respect that my unfolding journey is part of the mystery, and, as I evolve (as does each of us), the what-I-can-understand-for-now answers morph and evolve as well. I can only give you my accumulated, Source-inspired thoughts and knowing as of the writing of this book, all of which contribute to my personal mindset and guides this narrative. I hope it is productive and helpful to this conversation of transcendental leadership. After a lifetime of studying, meditating, deep listening, deep dialoguing, life experience, global travels, careers spanning both for-profit businesses and nonprofit endeavors, drawing upon spiritual guidance, and thorough personal inquiry and reflection, here, in simplistic terms, is my "take."

- Each of us is an aspect of Source. *Each one.* We are "God stuff," as I have said before. It can be no other way.

- Every*thing* is an aspect of Source as well. *Everything.* It can be no other way. Macrocosm to microcosm. The whole shebang.
- We are each unique selves, *one-of-a-kind expressions* of Source in this lifetime in the life forms we have been given.
- Source is *loving* us, *witnessing everything* and *every moment* with us, and expressing *through* us.
- Source only asks us to be our unique selves in expressing love and compassion, in serving the whole—each other and our beautiful world.

Frankly, it is as simple as that. We and everything are unique, interconnected expressions of Source. Therefore, as we tap into the frequency and state of transcendent awareness, we become more connected to *being* the expression of Source, love, and compassion.

It's a lofty notion. I know. However, I believe that the wisdom-bound and heart-centered leaders of today want to embrace and, to the best of their ability, embody this Source-inspired approach in their lifestyles and leadership.

I understand that in a book about leadership transcendence may sound a bit farfetched, especially to those who would prefer to remain complacently *asleep.* That being said, there is no doubt that our collective humanity is in the process of awakening to its higher potentials.

Integrated within the trait of understanding the true nature of reality are the ageless attributes of wisdom, awareness, and serving the whole.

Wisdom

In the context of the traits that a transcendental leader embodies, I define wisdom as the objective and subjective capacity to think, feel, act, and behave in a manner demonstrating knowledge, experiential insight, compassion, self-understanding, emotional balance, benevolence, and ethical values. The goal of wisdom is understanding yourself, humanity, and the nature of reality.

To know thyself is the beginning of wisdom.
—Socrates

Awareness

For the sake of our new narrative, awareness can be described as an increase in conscious presence. Present moment awareness allows for the objective inquiry, internal stillness, and introspection of your thoughts, feelings, and emotions. Being more present increases your self-awareness and is an avenue for deeper connection to others, our world around us, and the cosmos. The goal of awareness is to access higher states of consciousness.

To a mind that is still, the whole universe surrenders.
—Lao Tzu

Serves the Whole

The transcendental leader innately serves the whole. By this, I mean that they intuitively understand that the universe is interconnected. They perceive the world as a holographic field of Implicate Order and connectivity. They are aware of science and how we, along with everything else in the macrocosm and microcosm, are made up of the same "stuff." The goal of service to the whole is the manifestation of compassion, relationships, and a loving, meaningful life.

> *The best way to find yourself is to lose yourself in the*
> *service of others.*[1]
> —*Mohandas Gandhi*

Top Traits of Transcendental Leadership

Following are the top traits of transcendental leadership.

A transcendental leader accesses portals of expansive awareness. We'll talk about the various portals that can be used to create connection and relationship with Source in the next chapter. Portals are practices, like meditation or quality time in nature, that alter the practitioner's state. As far as we know, it is only through such primary gateways that individuals enhance their ability both to be informed by Source and to lead others with Source as their inherent guide.

During workshops and seminars that he leads, Peter Matthies utilizes many introspective practices to raise the consciousness of his participants. In an interview on transcendental leadership, he told me a story that exemplifies Source-inspired guidance.

It was in late September 2009 when I met with a friend and potential Conscious Business Institute partner at the beautiful Carneros Resort in Napa Valley. We had spent a couple of hours of inspiring conversation before I traveled on to my small boutique hotel in Napa to stay for the night. The

Californian evening sun was still warm, and I decided to go for a run through the Napa hillsides. As I ran, I felt an unusual flow—an unusual connection to the environment around me. It was as though my senses were sharpened; the trees, people, and even cars felt more vibrant and alive, and I, myself, felt a higher sense of sharpness, of aliveness. Although I was running up a hillside road, I didn't get exhausted. My body felt invigorated, and I kept running and running, feeling the warm evening sun on my skin.

When I returned back to my hotel, I sat by the pool as the sun was slowly setting. I heard a family chatting from the others side of the pool, but otherwise there was silence. When I decided to use the opportunity to meditate, still feeling the warmth of the Californian summer evening wash over my body, the connection I felt during my run deepened. For a moment, it seemed that it was just myself and the universe present, as though I had entered a space in which I was able to communicate with entities that were invisible to me—like a Zoom meeting for the soul, without the ability to see anyone, but with a strong sense of presence and belonging, as though my entire body was embraced by an invisible, timeless presence.

As I reflected on my earlier meeting, a question entered my mind: "What exactly differentiates a conscious business from a traditional one?" I, of course, had developed a sense of the difference, but never pinned it down to something that could be easily shared with others. As I allowed myself to relax into the question, a circle with four quadrants—like a pie cut into four equal pieces—entered my consciousness, and then, step-

71

by-step I experienced the outlining of each of the four pieces and its importance to the process of creating an inspired, well-functioning, conscious organization.

As I was lying on my poolside chair on this otherwise "ordinary" evening, I didn't grasp the power of this insight. When I opened my eyes, I immediately knew that there was something to it. My question had been answered. But my understanding was far from grasping how far this framework could reach into our societal structures—that what I just received could indeed become a framework, a model, for a better way to work and live. For over ten years now, this model has become the foundation for our work and has helped over 25,000 professionals in 160 countries around the world.[2]

A transcendental leader acknowledges a force at work throughout the cosmos. These leaders recognize the interdependence of a global society, intuitively sensing the implicate and interconnectedness of the whole, and desires to serve the whole. In Joseph Jaworski's book, *Source: The Inner Path of Knowledge Creation,* he reminds us of theoretical physicist and quantum philosopher David Bohm's work.

The totality of existence is enfolded within each fragment of space and time—whether it is a single object, thought, or event. Thus, everything in the universe, including human intentions and ways of being, affects everything else, because everything else is of the same unbroken whole.[3]

Although, we normally see our world as *us* and *them,* science clearly tells us that we are not separate but a symbiotic system of interconnected frequencies and energy. Transcendental leaders respect all life: all people, all creatures, all elements in the natural landscape, and the entire living system of our planet and the cosmos. Understanding the nature of the universe and its interconnectivity, they are in a natural flow, spontaneously witnessing opportunities coming and going, doors opening and doors closing. They practice the ability to surrender to what is while maintaining intention.

A transcendental leader values and expresses truth, moral ethics, trust, and authenticity. One of my all-time favorite quotes is by William Shakespeare. It is from Polonius' speech to Laertes in *Hamlet,* act 1, scene 3.

This above all: To thine own self be true.
And it must follow, as the night the day,
Thou canst not then be false to any man.

Although, as you may know, this statement can be understood in several ways, I feel that the trait of being true to thine own self is the call to be honest, authentic, genuine, and *self-aware.* A leader must be brave enough to be honest and speak the truth.

If "like attracts like," then why would anyone want to associate with and attract liars, the disingenuous, the manipulative, and the self-serving? An enlightened populace is aligned and attracted to truth, honesty, and integrity, which in turn elicits trust.

Truth spoken directly from the heart and from the source of wisdom illuminates and inspires. Therefore, be willing to look at your shadow side even if it's uncomfortable. We all have our personal shadows. It's the leaders who are brave enough and willing enough to take a deep inner dive to uncover their shadows who can come into the light to be seen, understood, and if need be, embraced and forgiven.

Bishop Heather Shea, CEO and Spiritual Director, United Palace of Spiritual Arts in New York City, says:

> *Transcendental leadership springs from an all-encompassing personal, ethical core and moral vision. They articulate a collective vision that promises to propel the people in and around their organizations to higher levels of moral living, ethical and social achievement, and collective evolution.*[4]

A transcendental leader has the capacity for joy and the ability to be playful. The energy field radiated by the optimistic and joyful individual is contagious. Judith Skutch Whitson, chairwoman of the board of directors of the Foundation for Inner Peace, the publishers of *A Course in Miracles,* shared with me an insight she had after she met the Dalai Lama.

> *Someone asked me, why am I laughing all the time? It's because I think everything is joyous and funny. Was I always like this? No, no, no, I wasn't. But when you follow a practice, it doesn't matter what it is ... Look at the Dalai Lama. I used to wonder why he laughs all the time. Now I know: He doesn't laugh about anything; he just laughs because he is imbued with bubbling gratitude!*
>
> *That was a major insight for me because earlier I had thought of the Dalai Lama as lofty and "way up there," considering he's one of the world's great spiritual leaders. But we're all capable of joy.*[5]

Roger Tempest, the custodian of Broughton Hall Estate and Avalon Wellbeing Centre in Yorkshire, England, and his partner, Paris Ackrill, cofounder and director at Avalon share:

A transcendental leader would be a person both connected to Source and the world in which they have chosen to incarnate. They are passionate about creating greater joy and wholeness in our relative world, and they draw inspiration from the absolute Source.[6]

A witty, relaxed, and healthy sense of humor is a bonus. There is something so wonderfully compelling and attractive in humor and a lighthearted, happy disposition. Reflect on your internal disposition of being.

A transcendental leader has a capacity to suspend certainty. If we think we know everything in a given situation, then we are unable to be open to previously unexplored potentials and realities. There is knowledge, wisdom, and guidance available that can foster far greater, more meaningful potentialities than we can imagine oftentimes or even dream of ourselves. We are living in uncertain times. It is quite challenging to suspend certainty and get comfortable with uncertainty. Becoming comfortable with uncertainty has been one of my biggest lessons through the various phases of the covid pandemic.

This element of suspension or certainty, or surrender, is akin to the Buddhist notion of nonattachment, and, as you have already learned, a core lesson in *The Bhagavad Gita* is not to be attached to the outcome. By suspending our attachment to outcomes, we can tap into an enhanced dimension of creativity allowing us to be open to new ideas, solutions, and innovative gifts that are oftentimes far greater than we could have ever thought of ourselves. A significant trait of transcendental leadership is practicing suspending judgment, preconceptions, and internal dialogue and surrendering control. Can you shift your perspective?

A transcendental leader expresses compassion and empathy. Having a genuine interest and caring for others contributes to a happy life. Such leaders cultivate the nurturing qualities of the feminine in themselves, such as empathy for others, sensitivity, gentleness, and warmth. They are unbiased and nonjudgmental and exhibit values that encourage diversity and the sharing of diverse, even oppositional, opinions. They are naturally open so that the people around them feel seen and heard.

A transcendental leader acts courageously. Such leaders are willing to stand up for what is right, to have the difficult conversation, and to bravely express their truth. In *Dare to Lead*, professor of research and business management Brené Brown, Ph.D., L.M.S.W., writes:

> *Courage is contagious. To scale daring leadership and build courage in teams and organizations, we have to cultivate a culture in which brave work, tough conversations, and whole hearts are the expectation, and armor is not necessary or rewarded. If we want people to fully show up, to bring their whole selves including their unarmored, whole hearts—so that we can innovate, solve problems, and serve people—we have to be vigilant about a culture in which people feel safe, seen, heard, and respected.[7]*

Courage takes bravery, self-awareness, and a desire to serve the whole.

A transcendental leader is creative. True originality is often a mystery. Where does the creative impulse come from? What triggers inspiration?

We are intrinsically creative beings. Creation is the natural process of life and evolution. It comes from openness to wonder, to not-knowing, and it's often brave; furthermore, as we know, it can arise from individuals whom we normally might describe as unstable. Some of the most inventive engineers, mathematicians, scientists, philosophers, and artists will tell you that their creative ideas come from an inner source.

Embracing our creativity and doing what we must to enhance the creative process is a touchstone to wisdom and thinking outside the box. Creativity is the capacity to translate intuitive hunches, visions, and ideas/images that arise from Source into solid intentions and goals that guide our actions and manifestations. This trait allows the deeper territory of creativity to emerge and unfold.

Artist Judi Weisbart, president and founder of A Busy Woman Consulting, is passionate about her creativity. In conversation with me, she shared how alive creativity is in her life, and how she believes the artistic process provides all of us with lessons in understanding ourselves and others.

My blessing in life is that I am a creative. My passion is to get lost or enter the space of the creator and make art. The mediums I use are mainly from the Earth: stone, wood, and clay. I am a sculptor and I love the feeling of partnership with these natural substances to create another thing.

When I was younger, I carved stone and, when I did, I knew that it wanted me to listen to what it wanted to become. If I ignored it, it might shatter. If I listened, I learned the patience to be a better sculptor and a better mother, wife, friend, and human being. Now, I do more clay pieces and clay teaches me that life is process. It needs more than one firing to make it strong. Even those of us who start out weak, soft, fragile become strong vessels of import after going through enough firings!

We all come from the same Earth and I believe that art is one of my portals into that place of connection and communication with the world.[8]

A transcendental leader cultivates emotional balance. When leaders cultivate emotional balance, they can remain centered when emotionally triggered and are able to respond calmly, thoughtfully, respectfully, and practically. They have social and self-awareness, perceiving group dynamics, reading the emotions of others, and expressing talent for managing relationships and overall patience.

To develop this trait yourself, learn to understand yourself in order to make distinctions between logical, rational, pragmatic decisions and gut reactions based on your default fears and ego-based psychological triggers. Learning to take a mindful pause to step back, as it were, will allow you to be more aware of what's driving you in your interactions.

This trait also includes the capacity for work/life balance. Stephan Rechtschaffen, cofounder of the Omega Institute for Holistic Studies in Rhinebeck, New York, and of the Blue Spirit

Retreat Center in Nosara, Costa Rica, shared with me his take on this and a personal experience.

We're a world out of balance, and certainly this has been happening in the world of leadership as well, because what has occurred is we have leadership that strives and tries to always be growing, whereas nature naturally grows. It comes after a natural ebb and flow of times of being fallow. It's the yin and the yang, the moon and the sun, the balancing point of energies. Transcendence recognizes this whole, yet we've lost our true sense of balance.

When I look out into the world these days, I don't see the leadership of any large country in the world leading from a point of view of wisdom or a point of deep understanding. Unfortunately, it's the perspective of the notion that success requires continuous material growth: growth for the sake of growth. This collective worldview of the larger countries in the world is clearly out of balance, and it's why we're so out of balance with nature.

I feel that finding this balance in everyday life is where transcendence happens. For me, it's the melding of meditation, where it becomes nondual, yet aligned with the heart, the mind, and the felt body, which is the true sense of what the Tibetans call the subtle body. *Transcendental leadership embodies all of that.*

I can give an example in my own life of when I was asked to start a new project at the time when I was working with Omega. I successfully created Omega from the early 1970s and it was growing well. Somebody asked me to spearhead a new, big, longevity center, located about two hours from where

I was living at the time. And there was all this promise of "This is going to be great. We're going to make a lot of money."

I was in the nonprofit world and I was attracted by all this: It's going to be great *talk; but really, I could feel the pressure of it all, and one day I was driving to the project and I took my fist and hit it into the steering wheel as I was driving. I said,* Stephan, don't do this project. *There was that gut feeling that this wasn't what I should be doing. However, I went ahead and did the project.*

And not through any fault of our own (it was the financial times), it went bankrupt.

*But my deep learning was that it wasn't right for me. It wasn't the right project because it was not balanced in the kind of transcendent way that your book (*Transcendental Leadership*) is about. The project wasn't seen from the whole. There were certain aspects that attracted me in our world then, the aspects of having wealth, the aspects of having power, the aspects of having all of these more "male" attributes, let's say. Leadership, as the sole head of something, tends to be what people emulate, and, at the time, there I was doing that.*

It was a great lesson. I remember discovering that your chance for enlightenment becomes far greater when you go bankrupt than when you win a million dollars; it is much greater when you lose a lot in your life, rather than when you acquire a lot in your life.

So, for me, these were some deep lessons along the way of recognizing that what moved me and what still moves me is not money and it's not growth, it's about creating something that has deep holistic value.[9]

A transcendental leader engages in deep listening and dialogue with others. One of the many benefits of the twelve months of pandemic lockdown, March 2020 to March 2021, was the practical experience of daily solitude, which caused us to be more introspective and thoughtful and to deeply listen *inwardly* to ourselves. If nothing else, we had to be with the tumultuous cacophony of our own thoughts.

Obviously, there is both the listening to others and the listening to oneself: that deep, inner voice within. In this context of traits, I'm referring here to the capacity to deeply listen to another. A person develops deeper wisdom through attentive, deep listening, and dialogue.

Susan Taylor, cofounder and CEO of Generon International, often muses:

The fact that the English words listen *and* silent *contain the same letters is no coincidence to me. Our obstacles to listening are our preconceived notions and the attachments we have to them. With these beliefs come hard, fast assumptions and expectations that build up our individual sense of need to get our ideas out there—through words. And if we don't, somehow, we will get lost or not be noticed, our leadership weakened. This is where something as simple as an intentional pause can be incredibly profound and what dialogue has the power to create: A space to connect with our assumptions, expectations, and points of view—not to defend them—but to hold them.*

When we defend, we cannot possibly listen. In holding, we create the container to first understand others before projecting our understanding on to them. Transcendental

81

leaders deeply recognize this need for pause and know silence to be the central feature *to deep listening and the essence of dialogue itself.*[10]

If you wish to develop this trait yourself, learn to ask thoughtful, probing questions with authentic curiosity. Diane Marie Williams, founder and president of the Source of Synergy Foundation, says:

I have no doubt that this form of nonlocal communication that involves suspending our old worldviews for the new, through deep listening, a welcoming heart, and a belief that there are many dimensions of existence, is the key to successful transcendental leadership.[11]

Bishop Heather Shea says:

Deep listening means knowing what you do not know and holding what you are convinced you know lightly. Deep listening requires a willingness to truly hear, to grow, and at times even to change. It requires a profound respect for others and other possibilities.[12]

A transcendental leader empowers others and champions their self-growth. These leaders encourage, cultivate, and have an honest desire to contribute to the heart, mind, body, and soul of others. Generally, they are healthier, wiser, happier, more connected, and desire to be of service. They inspire their constituents to pursue altruistic goals—like a vision, dream, ideology, or purpose. They deliberately and readily give credit to their colleagues and team members. Empowering, nurturing, and supporting their colleagues and employees generates loyalty and respect.

A transcendental leader practices gratitude. There is a lot written today about the benefits of both feeling and expressing sincere gratitude. Being grateful is an indicative byproduct of wisdom and awareness. Around 2015, when I was working for the La Casa de Maria Retreat Center in Montecito, California, we had the wonderful opportunity to host psychologist and integrative medicine pioneer Joan Borysenko, Ph.D., and have her conduct a women's weekend conference and retreat with us. I remember her telling the group about her gratitude practice, which sounded so great that I adopted it. I continue to use it to this day.

Here's the instruction. Each day, pick *one* thing to be grateful for. And the trick is that you can't repeat that thing . . . meaning, each day you have to be grateful for something *new*. Before you know it, you will become more *mindful* throughout the day, seeing the world through the lens of gratitude.

A transcendental leader has an intrinsic mindset of generosity. Leaders with a grateful mindset are generous with acknowledgment, time, energy, feedback, and support, as well as offering appropriate fiscal compensation and benefits to the people who work with them. Many organizations have come to light in the last few years that overwork and underpay their employees.

I myself once worked for a nonprofit that did not have a mindset of generosity towards most of its employees. Sadly, a historical, collective parsimonious philosophy permeated the organization, deeply affecting the employees and causing an often dispirited morale despite the good works the staff was accomplishing.

On the other hand, I have also consulted for a nonprofit with a mindset of enormous generosity. The owners and founders were both financially and emotionally supportive to those who worked at every level of the organization.

The difference in the true joy, productivity, and wellbeing between the staffs of these two organizations were like night and day.

A transcendental leader has humility. This trait is personified by a diminished sense of personal ego. Such leaders feel no need for self-aggrandizement. They are aware of their strengths and weaknesses.

Judith Skutch Whitson, describing the work of publishing *A Course in Miracles*, told me:

> *I felt I was given a holy trust, a sacred trust, and I would let the same voice that dictated the course, which was also inside of me, tell me what to do. I was constantly reminded, from the very beginning of one of the lines in the Course that I love so much: "I will step back and let him lead the way. I will step back and let him lead the way."*[13]

Transcendental leaders walk their talk, are modest about their accomplishments, and have nothing-to-prove demeanors. Such people are transparent and learn from and take responsibility for their mistakes. They do their best not to take things personally. They are comfortable with shared decision making and are willing to seek advice from trusted and knowledgeable peers and experts.

I asked Peter Matthies how he bridges his business and conscious awareness. He shared:

In an ideal world, when I am leading from a higher, universal consciousness, there's no bridging between business and spiritual reality necessary. All decisions are informed by the spiritual reality because business becomes an expression of spirit. However, in the real world, when I, as a leader, lose my connection to a universal consciousness on a given day as I get exposed to daily business or relationship issues, like any other human being, I use two practices to bridge my business activities and my spiritual awareness: First, I aim to continuously practice and check in whether I am operating from a sense of fear or scarcity, or whether my decisions are made from a place of interconnectedness and abundance, and second, to clean up after myself whenever I've communicated, decided, or operated from a place of disconnection, I go back to the people I impacted with my behaviors and speak to them.[14]

In this remark, Peter is showcasing for us a leader willing to face a shadow/fear experience who is confident in their willingness to be humble and authentic.

A transcendental leader is inspiring and visionary. Leaders exemplifying the traits that I've described throughout this chapter motivate, encourage, and empower their teams and organizations. Their inner wisdom and passionate sense of purpose inspires their colleagues to altruistic and visionary goals, dreams, and ideologies.

One story that also illustrates this process was told to me by Joseph Jaworski, author of the books *Source, Presence,* and

Synchronicity. He explained that after he envisioned what the American Leadership Forum could do, it took him another seven years to gather the courage to leave the law firm where he was working.

> *Starting the Leadership Forum was something that I could not* not *do. It was just too important to me. I was going to do this no matter what happened. However, I was also fearful because I had no clue how to do it. I knew the dream was so big, it was going to take a lot more money than I had. I was going to have to raise the money. But first of all, I was going to have to figure out a curriculum. How do you do this?*
>
> *It was that kind of commitment that allowed me to walk away from everything I'd built for twenty years. That's the kind of commitment, which then, magically, opened the doors for me. It was as if, as Joseph Campbell says, supernatural forces came to assist me.*
>
> *I started working on a curriculum, trying to write this and that, but hitting a wall. One day, I went out and took a long run in Hyde Park. I ran for three or four hours and came back after daybreak. And on the front steps of my little flat was the Sunday edition of the* New York Times. *I picked it up, took it inside, and was lying on the floor stretching. I threw the paper down and miraculously, automatically it opened to a headline that read: "Wholeness and the Implicate Order." I had no clue what that meant specifically, but it spoke to me, spoke to my body, and in my heart I knew that this was important. I stopped my stretching and started reading it.* "Oh my God," *I thought,* this is the answer to everything I'm seeking. This is how I could form the curriculum!

I got up and ran to the phone. I think it was 7:30 or 8:00 A.M. This article was about an important new book that David Bohm had just written. Boldly, I tried to reach him and miraculously, I finally got him after several calls. I don't even remember exactly what I said, but it was full of energy and passion and intention because it was compelling enough to him where he said, "Mr. Jaworski, I'm going to cancel everything I have tomorrow. Meet me in my office at 10:00."

I spent the next day with him there and that meeting changed my life.

That's how I wrote those three books all on topics which Bohm taught me about that day. And that was the beginning of the American Leadership Forum.[15]

A transcendental leader is intuitive and insightful. The ability to tap into and listen to greater intuitive *awareness* increases our ability for organic, clear perception and understanding of a situation or a problem. Known as the sixth sense, intuitive awareness involves acute observations and discernment that can seemingly come out of nowhere. It is the intrinsic capacity to be attuned with universal wisdom and the Implicate Order, so that what wants to emerge emerges.

Catherine Butler, owner of the charming and renowned At the Chapel, a restaurant and retreat property located in the English countryside of Somerset, England, shared with me her understanding of intuition.

Our intuition is downloaded from another realm and all exploration begins with intuition. These discoveries expand our understanding of who we really are and lead us to a deeper understanding of ourselves. The answers lie within.[16]

Esperide Ananas Ametista, spokesperson for the Temples of Humankind in Piedmont, Italy, believes in the power of intuition to guide us. She told me:

Insights coming from our dreams are also important. This is a field of research, training and study. Ancient, secret knowledge on dreaming is now becoming available—be it from ancient Tibet, Mexico, or the tradition of Damanhur, where I live. It invites us to enter a more expansive and complex reality, than the one we normally know. We cannot walk the paths of the world of dreams as amateurs. Its different doors open to those who commit to refining their senses, through a love for Nature, Beauty and appreciation of every sensory experience; those who perfect their relationship with Life and Spirit cultivating gratitude and learning to master their breathing; and those who study, study and study more. Last, but not least, all wisdom traditions tell us, the best dreams are dreamt in community: a transcendental leader cannot become such without a sincere, open and conscious interaction with other people.[17]

A transcendental leader is receptive to knowledge. Not just the knowledge of a subject in terms of facts and data, but the capacity to be open to an inner, deeper knowledge and wisdom, which combines pragmaticism with intuitive knowing. Being open to new perspectives allows for innovation, visionary endeavors, and creative, paradigm-shifting downloads to occur.

A transcendental leader is present. This kind of present moment awareness automatically provides leaders the capacity for nonjudgmental observation, deep listening, and authentic dialogue. Presence also helps others feel that they're in an emotionally supportive and safe environment to express themselves honestly, be out-of-the-box creative, share their challenges, and to seek, engage with, and provide thoughtful, honest feedback.

The quality of presence contributes to an increase in knowing, like what Wildrik Timmerman, cofounder of the Mandali Retreat Center, shared with me in an interview.

It's hard to talk about presence without sounding as if I think I know anything about it. Whereas the truth is that I am just learning. Every day. I feel that when I am in deep presence, knowing happens. It's not so much that I have to obtain information, the information is just there. It's about being open to it, "knowing" it. When intuition happens, it's beautiful. But also, many times, it does not happen. At least, not when I want it. And that's just the point. Not wanting. Wanting is of the mind. Knowing is of the heart.[18]

A transcendental leader is purpose driven. Such leaders have a passion for meaning and purpose. Showcasing this trait is a leader that is passionately drawn to a purpose that ignites them, inspires others, and is in *service to the whole.* Philosophical theologist Jim Garrison, Ph.D., founder and president of Ubiquity University, explains:

Transcendence influences your choices. For example, if I wasn't a yoga practitioner and a dedicated meditator, I could have easily ended up in politics in a secular kind of way. But I think the more you engage in spiritual practice, the more spiritualized your life becomes, and as a result I ended up founding Ubiquity University and the Chartres Academy in Chartres, France, which is its mystery school. If I look back on my life, I think that when you really bring the transcendence in, it influences your orientation to what livelihood is the most appropriate to you. And that's very important. I think I'm doing what I'm doing today in my life because I've had a strong spiritual practice essentially all of my adult life.[19]

A transcendental leader is resilient. Resilience is an inner, strength-of-character trait that provides a foundation supporting leaders to be flexible and adaptable. They persevere, are patient and aware, and can welcome all that arises. Clinical psychologist and Depth Psychology Chair at the Pacifica Graduate Institute, Juliet Rohde-Brown, Ph.D., says,

I try to be consistent with how I show up in life regardless of the context. Thus, how I might respond to, say, a conflictual situation in my organizational setting is congruent with how I respond in my marriage or other interpersonal relationships. I find an inner resilience when I slow down and breathe into my heart center. In this way, I can feel into an energetic intention of each of our hearts connecting at the subtle level. When I do this, there is a visceral shift and grounding in my body while at the same time opening to a kind of expansiveness.

I engage in meditative practices that nurture an impartial beneficence for all beings. In this way, I can pick myself up

90

with compassion when I make mistakes and I build my resilience and capacity to stay in a place of compassion with those who may even commit egregious acts, while not condoning those acts. I look to the context, not just the content. I see this as a continual learning as I stumble along the path of life in my humanness. Thus, I value the concept of beginner's mind and practices that cultivate more spaciousness of mind and heart.

We all have shadow aspects as well, so it is how we meet them that makes all the difference in our interpersonal interactions whether these relationships be personal or professional.[20]

A transcendental leader is responsible and accountable. Anyone who wants to be a respected and beloved leader understands that being responsible and accountable to consequences is fundamental. They govern themselves and, innately, follow the Eightfold Path of Buddhism. This includes awareness, boundaries, and a certain amount of self-discipline. Also, they do not blame others for their decisions and actions.

A transcendental leader values simplicity and regenerative sustainability. Culturally, we are learning that nonstop consumerism is both a self-induced and a collectively induced trap. People are awakening to the fact that following the dictates of the marketing machine of the advertising industry, which has been telling us for years that we are "not enough" unless we buy the next this-or-that, does not make us happy. Thoughtless consumerism and the mindless activity of shopping/buying will never fill the void of underlying psychological issues. Fortunately, a lot of us are choosing to live more simply and to consume less. Recycling is becoming the norm almost the world over. Smaller houses and electric cars are becoming increasingly popular. The trait of simplicity in a leader not only is good for them and their organization, but for their community. They are a role model to their family and community, showcasing service to the whole.

As mentioned, the core traits needed for understanding the true nature of the universe are, in essence, awareness, wisdom, and serving the whole. Transcendental leaders have a Source-inspired approach to living and leading. The attributes I've listed are the byproducts. They are foundational to the *being* of the individual leader, who models them, shares them, and cultivates them within their family, community, organization, country, and the world at large.

In the next chapter, we'll look at the various methods that are in alignment with Source —which I call *portals*—for accessing states of wisdom, awareness, and serving the whole. If you aspire to become a transcendental leader, one or more of these methods will be your primary portals.

REFLECTION EXERCISE

Before we move on, let's reflect for a few minutes. Take a moment to discern your own capacities and traits associated with transcendental leadership.

- Do you recognize many of these capacities within yourself?
- How many of these traits are in balance for you?
- Which ones would you most want to develop within yourself?
- Which ones would you like to discuss with your employees or team leaders?
- Which ones might be your strengths?
- Which ones might need further work on your part?

IV

PORTALS TO BEING A TRANSCENDENTAL LEADER

I am awake.
—Buddha

What is the journey from the sleeping state to the awakened state? From ignorance to awareness?

Where are the doorways to self-knowledge and harmonious connection to the wisdom of the unified field of the cosmos?

What can we do to increase the moments and circumstances in our lives that are opportune for propelling us into new and transformational mindsets and numinous states of being—ones attuned to and aligned with the flow and universal wisdom of Source?

What are the guiding practices necessary and available for becoming a transcendental leader?

Portals and Practices

We can find nuggets of profound wisdom arising from silence and deep listening to our own inner voices. Each of us has a source of divinity within us. Such insights may also emerge when we earnestly study sacred wisdom scriptures, such as *The Bhagavad Gita* or *The Bible,* and stories like that of the Buddha's deep inquiry sitting under the Bodhi tree or Jesus Christ's forty days and forty nights alone in the desert, or even accounts from recent history, such as the incarceration of Nelson Mandela, the former president of South Africa, who spent many years in prison (often in solitary confinement) during the Apartheid era in that nation.

Scientific studies and sociological research indicate that certain disciplined practices, when kept up over time, will produce changes in the brain and body that provide the practitioner with greater levels of awareness, connection, and deep knowing. These practices include forms of meditation and contemplative prayer, quality time spent in nature, the Four Paths of Yoga, expressing yourself creatively through arts such as painting and music, and active movement such as qigong and dance, among others. What is required to become a transcendental leader is a consistent commitment to a disciplined practice for *becoming awakened.*

Theoretical physicist and philosopher David Bohm once said that within every individual is a "gateway to a remarkable wealth of unexpected information" *if* a "consistent and deep" personal practice is established.[1] Portals of awareness are key to developing the being of a transcendental leader, someone attuned to deep states of wisdom and with a heart and mindset of service to the whole—consisting of individuals, organizations, institutions, communities, nations, and our planet.

Just as there are different ways that each of us learns best, which vary from person to person, so too there are different access points to transcendence that resonate with different people. Each of us has unique preferences. We resonate with and align to one portal and practice over another.

Let me share what I mean. Consider people who go to church every Sunday morning, believing that their attendance connects them to God even if they may be typically inattentive during the service. If they are not mentally present, nothing is feeding their souls.

Let's say that the same day these same people walk to the beach and go surfing. The afternoon feels exhilarating—they savor the fresh air, the sunshine, the glistening sea, the soft sand. And, while surfing, at a certain moment, they experience a ride inside the green room—the sweet spot inside the curl of a wave—peeking, peaking, and piquing *transcendence.* Existentially, they feel a numinous unity with the sea *and all of nature.*

That's the bliss of a real holy moment—not a prescribed practice but an experiential awareness.

I think that each of us has more than one portal to access the transcendent, and it's important to honor yourself by discovering the right portals for you.

Additionally, keep an open mind. Assume that your preferences could change over your lifespan.

As a girl and younger woman, I was athletic and enjoyed many sports. When I was horseback riding, waterskiing or snow skiing, I discovered that combining nature and movement was a portal of transcendence for me. For example, because I was a confident rider, I could both control and surrender to my horse running through the wide, yet evergreen tree-lined trails in the Pacific Northwest. Sublime, strong and utterly blissed out, I was in a child's fantasy of Heaven-on-Earth. Additionally, as a good skier, I could ski full out and surrender to the flow of swiftly skimming over the water or the snow. I could smell, see, and feel the warm water spray in the summer or the crispy cold snow in the winter. Depending on where I was (once, when I was waterskiing in Tonga, I became one with the sea and the spectacular crepuscular rays of a brilliant sunset . . . *nirvana*), I could immerse myself in the visual grandeur and cosmic presence of Gaia, Mother Nature—perhaps witnessing a vista of snowcapped mountains touching the sky or a horizon of sparkling sunlight refracting upon the water. No thinking was involved in the combined portal of movement and nature. I was immersed in a transcendent holy moment and if anything, thinking, *This feels like Heaven.*

Along this vein, I will endeavor in this chapter to showcase various portals of transcendence, giving you categories with brief descriptions and bullet points to get you thinking. In addition, I've chosen to group them by related practices. You may notice that they overlap with each other in some instances.

If one of these portals resonates strongly with you, I encourage you to engage in deeper research of it and inquiry. Take the time to find the portals that access transcendence for you. You will discover the ones that are right for you. They are the gateways that can provide you alignment to Source, deep joy, peace, awareness, and wisdom.

At the end of the chapter, I'm including a few questions that might help you discover your primary portals. As a caveat, these portals are not listed in any order of priority.

Let's explore the portals of:

- Nature,
- Meditation and contemplation,
- Movement,
- Creativity,
- Relationship,
- Devotion,
- Inspired writings,
- Service,
- Knowing,
- Indigenous wisdom,
- Yoga.

The Portal of Nature

What do you think of the world of nature and its "aliveness" all over the globe? We have already touched upon the accepted scientific understanding that Planet Earth is a single, interconnected, holistic living system with its own consciousness as opposed to an inanimate object that is not a living organism and doesn't have a conscious element to it. The Gaia hypothesis postulated by chemist James Lovelock and microbiologist Lynn Margulis in the 1970s is that our planet is self-regulating.[2]

If you're like most people, no doubt you have experienced moments of transcendence in a natural setting. Anyone pondering the meaning of life should spend time in a garden or wilderness area. There are profound reasons as to why gardens are considered sacred spaces as well as central themes in the sacred scriptures of the world's greatest religions: A garden has always been the kind of place where the soul goes to rest, wonder, play, meditate, grieve, and refresh. As part of a connected cosmic organism, we are engaged in a multilayered dance with the entire biosphere of Earth, with plants, sunlight, animals, birds, flowers, bees, butterflies, rainbows, fragrance, and a cast of thousands of microorganisms. Mother Nature has at its heart, the presence of Source. The more contact we can have with nature, the more aware we can be of our oneness with all.

Diane Marie Williams, aligns with nature to support her leadership. She says:

Whenever I have an important meeting, have to write an article, or need to offer some words on an online program, I often take some time prior to be in nature and deeply listen for insights regarding what is most needed. Experiencing the loving support one receives when opening up to these portals often evokes a pure sense of existential awe, joy and lightness of being. The gift to be in deeper coherence with the totality of existence is a gift that keeps on giving.[3]

How often have you felt a symbiotic and numinous connection amid the trees of a forest or while floating on the lake, sea or ocean? Quiet time in a natural setting, whether it is in a canyon or your own backyard, is one of the most common and important portals for connecting to Source.

I was fortunate to spend my childhood growing up in a semirural, lakefront setting in the Pacific Northwest of the United States. Our house was surrounded by forests in which to make trails and build forts and simple campsites alongside thickets of wild blackberry brambles whose fruit we could gobble on in the summer. There also was a big lake (Lake Washington) to swim in endlessly. Sometimes I would just stretch out on our dock, close my eyes, and listen to the happy slap slip slop of choppy water against the pilings while feeling the light, wispy caress of a breezy north wind upon my face turned up towards the warm sun. The perfect peek-peak-pique moments of childhood were good training for effortlessly surrendering to the comforting and peaceful connection with Mother Nature.

Historically, members of Indigenous cultures that lived on undeveloped land in a symbiotic relationship with nature (before we called it "real" estate) understood this same connection both physically and spiritually. Nowadays, it's

101

popular for business leaders to partake in teambuilding and self-reliance courses with their colleagues and employees through programs like vision quests that take people on adventures in untamed landscapes.

Hippos, Flamingos, and the Presence of Gaia

In 1990, I was on a camping safari in Kenya with my husband at the time. We were on a customized trip with three friends and had planned a couple of days at a camp lodge located on Ol Kokwe, a small island in the middle of Lake Baringo. The camp-lodge consisted of a small cluster of charming individual cabins with one main lodge where we ate our meals. As I recall, this was nestled near the top of the island, with all the small, thatched-roofed cabins fringed about the property overlooking Lake Baringo.

The day before, we had made our way there in two Range Rovers with our guides along the lakeshore of Lake Nakuru, which is renowned for the millions of teeming flamingos. It was an extraordinary site/sight. Imagine the plumage of hundreds and hundreds of thousands of flamingos, creating a coral blush sea that extended for miles and miles. I stood up in the truck as we sped along the shore, feeling the rush of the wind on my face as I was witnessing the spectacular grandeur of salmon pink, feathered bodies, emerald-green shores, and azure water melding with the sky. For a longtime meditator who finds a portal to states of transcendence in nature, the sensation of the wisps of wind on my face felt like they had formed a halo around my body of bliss. I half closed my eyes and fell into a one-with-Gaia numinous trance not realizing that the best was yet to come.

Eventually, in the evening, when it had become dark, we arrived at Lake Baringo and took a couple of small motorboats over to the island, where we got settled in our cabins. The next day, we took a low-sided canoe out to meander along the lakeshore and surreptitiously observe the extraordinary variety of birds that inhabited the region and found many hippos happily bobbing in the water. Obviously, we did our best to stay clear of the hippos, which are large, sometimes ferocious animals, but sometimes they were difficult to notice except when pointed out by our guides. They barely had their eyes above the water, making them difficult to discern through the verdant foliage and colorful water plants floating on the top of the water by the shore. Every once in a while, the hippos would raise their giant snouts and snort at us! Whoa! Keep clear!

But the birds—oh, the birds! —were less intimidating. There was such an array of avian diversity: One species of eagle had long beaks for fishing. Other birds had long, spindly legs that evolved for tiptoeing among the reedy shore weeds and brilliant feathers to showcase themselves to hopeful mates. The lake birds of Kenya are an ornithologist's dream! The birdlife in Africa is often overlooked in comparison to many of the other marvelous creatures at home on the continent, however the birds there are truly spectacular. How often do we truly pause to ponder and wonder at the exquisite array of wildlife that has evolved on our planet?

That evening, after my husband and I and our friends spent time by the pool relaxing and had then cleaned ourselves up, we decided to go have cocktails before dinner in the lodge. I told the others that I would "be there in a little while . . . I'm going to meditate first." Our cabin had a veranda that overlooked the lake on which there were two Adirondack-style chairs made from bamboo and reeds. I grabbed a blanket (it wasn't cold, it just felt cozier) and scooch-settled on one of the chairs with the soft "blankie" around my shoulders.

The sun was setting, and there was a pink-gold hue shimmering on Lake Baringo's surface. I could see a few local fishermen in their canoes returning home. It was a quiet, peaceful time of day. You know, when the cadence of the day's activities and your circadian rhythm sync you and every other living being around you with a restful, ending-of-the-day serenity with the sunset.

I settled into a slightly morphed version of Transcendental Meditation, which, as I mentioned, I learned while a student at the University of Washington in Seattle during my hippie-academic phase. Thinking I would meditate for twenty minutes and then meet everyone for drinks and dinner, I closed my eyes and centered my thoughts on my mantra. After about ten minutes, I could sense something different, a gentle, palpable vibration like an inner fluttering of the soul.

I recentered and dove in. As my sense of the outer world dropped away, my inner self expanded. At the same time, I oddly felt compelled to open my eyes. I half-opened them to gently gaze upon the reflections of the light and dark in the early night scene. In the natural garden, I could see/sense the silhouette of the trees against the lake beyond and I noticed a small iguana creeping in the grass. The Spirit of Gaia caressed and enveloped me like a mist. My perception of reality was shifting and I was on the verge of an otherworldly vision. I was both excited and a little frightened.

Gently the holy moment expanded and I *did* experience a vision. But it wasn't something otherworldly . . . I witnessed

God/Source in nature. I saw It. I felt It. I was It. I was completely absorbed and connected to a world shimmering in an all-embracing love-dance. Colors and light sparkled around me like crystalline stars and dewdrops. The trees, shrubs, grass, and flowers merged with the sky and lake and stars and yet remained distinct. My body gently pulsated in rhythm with the cosmos.

Unaware, soft tears seeped from the corners of my eyes. I rested in an ethereal awe.

Meanwhile, on the upper terrace of the main lodge, my husband and friends were beginning to wonder what happened to me. When was I going to join them? They had finished a round or two of cocktails and ambled into the dining area. When I finally floated into the dining area, eyes glazed over from my new perception of reality, my friends and husband could only think, *Where has she been?!*

I've never forgotten that numinous experience. Not just the sensing of my oneness with nature, but truly, visually seeing and feeling my being and nature raptly immersed together. I was aligned and one with everyone, everything, and all of the cosmos.

What I call nature's portal to a state of transcendence is available to everyone.

This portal includes:

- Vison quests.
- Forest bathing.
- Gardening.
- Sounds of the environment like the rustling of trees and babbling of water.
- The sacred frequency-sound of the cosmos: Aum.

- Spending time with our wild and domestic animal friends. This may be why primatologist Jane Goodall became a leader in the conservation and animal welfare movements. *"The least I can do is speak out for those that cannot speak for themselves."*[4]

The Portal of Meditation and Contemplation

The word *contemplation* comes from the Latin root *contemplatio*— meaning, "to gaze attentively" or "the act of looking upon." Just as scientists conduct experiments with technology, contemplatives conduct experiments using their silent perception and enhanced awareness. Meditation is similar. Through contemplation and meditation, we can begin to objectively view the full tumult of our conscious awareness and the contents of our perception: sights, sounds, sensations, thoughts, intentions, and emotions.

Our minds are ever-so-gushing-along with thoughts that randomly trail after each other. They spew thoughts that often extrapolate and take on their own meaning, psychology, emotions, and associations. All of this activity can create mental "rush hour traffic," as the renowned Buddhist teacher B. Alan Wallace, Ph.D., puts it.[5]

Because we are not monitoring or even aware of many of these thoughts and inner conversations, our ignorance misconstrues the thoughts. Before you know it, our thoughts are in control, rather than us controlling them. Contemplative practices provide us with the kind of self-awareness such that we may objectively and mindfully be present and aware of our thoughts (along with our perceptions, viewpoints, feelings, and so on), so that they can be viewed as mere phenomena flowing in and out of our consciousness.

Spiritual awareness/awareness of Source is not immediately evident in ordinary consciousness. Having a contemplative practice in their toolbox of life skills helps transcendental leaders to develop greater awareness by providing access to the expansive inner silence, out-of-the-box creativity, calming emotional balance, and insightful wisdom.

Meditation

Although I have been a longtime practitioner of TM and continue to stay somewhat aligned to this form of meditation, there are other forms of meditation I admire, and which you might prefer, such as mindfulness meditation, *metta* (loving-kindness) meditation, Kriya yoga (which includes recitation of mantras and divine names, hand postures known as *mudras,* and *pranayama,* or patterned breathing practices), Tonglen, and Zen meditation, to name but a few. An important purpose of any style of meditation is to become more conscious, aware, and familiar with the inner self.

Although there may be no definitive agreement on which technique of meditation is the best, countless research studies have been done that proves the benefits of meditative practices. Popular film director and longtime TM practitioner David Lynch, who established a foundation to disseminate TM as widely as possible, says:

> *We know that in one human being, when you ramp up consciousness—when you ramp up that light of unity— negative things begin to recede. In that individual, you see*

more and more intelligence, more and more creativity, more and more bliss, negativity going away, and a positive influence pouring out into the world. You've got this potential, but you're not going to get it unless you experience transcendence—at the deepest level. Pure consciousness. And every time you experience the transcendent, you infuse some of it and you grow in that consciousness. You grow in intelligence, creativity, happiness, love, energy, and peace.[6]

Meditation is referred to as a *practice* because it is an exercise for every individual to do regularly. It is unusual for the practitioner to achieve significant benefits in the first few weeks, although this can happen. It needs to be a part of your daily routine and, as any good coach, teacher, tutor, or trainer would tell you, you must keep practicing. In addition, I personally think it is important for the novice to begin with a bona fide teacher. Winging it after reading an article or a book won't be as effective or as enduring as learning from a reputable teacher.

A popular practice today in the West is mindfulness meditation. This practice of becoming intently aware of what's occurring in the present moment is a central teaching of Buddhism. It has been adapted by western teachers and become a popular mainstream form of meditation. Therapists also teach it to their clients as a technique to help them quell anxiety. One of the early pioneers of mindfulness in the United States is Jon Kabat-Zinn, a molecular biologist, educated at MIT, who began utilizing mindfulness to help people with chronic pain.

The core practice that quiets the individual's "chattering" mind is a sitting meditation wherein you close your eyes, focus on your breath, and notice each moment, then let it slip away as you mindfully notice the *next moment*.

Mindfulness, as do other forms of meditation, helps us to connect with a calm and deeper place within ourselves. Plus, the brain becomes retrained and is less mindlessly sucked into pointless ruminations, which are so often the source of stress and depressive thinking.

Peter Russell, author of *Letting Go of Nothing*, does very brief meditations. In his interview with me he shared:

Most of my practice these days is what I call micro-meditations. Pausing for a few moments, many times a day. Pausing whatever thought trains I may be following, allow myself to relax and notice how it feels to pause. Noticing what is here in the present moment. And aware of that transcendent essence, aware that I Am that which is aware of all this. Of course, my mind soon kicks in again, but it's not about trying to stay there, but returning many times.[7]

Like Peter, as often as possible, throughout my day, I remember, pause, and drop in to present awareness. My name for these is *holy moments*. And, you can have those holy moments just by taking a minute, a second, a timeout in your doing. When I pause for a holy moment, I can feel my frequency and energy shift. And, like a tuning fork, it creates and attracts like-energies in my Source field. *Anyone* can do this.

Bishop Shea agrees.

I lead a global spiritual center and one of New York's largest and most spectacular theaters and entertainment and education venues. Every moment is a moment of practice, a moment to listen and learn to be open to a full transformative encounter with individuals and the universe.[8]

Contemplation and Centering Prayer

Contemplative prayer is a form of practice that stems from the Christian tradition. It is often utilized in conjunction with Lectio Divina, which is listening to the texts of Christian scripture and "centering into communion" with the words of Jesus. Centering prayer is primarily based on the wisdom of Jesus' teaching in his famous Sermon on the Mount (Matthew 6:6), when he says:

But when you pray, go to your inner room, close the door and pray to your Father in secret. And your Father, who sees everything that is done in secret will reward you.[9]

Centering prayer is also inspired by other Christian contemplatives and mystics, such as St. John of the Cross, St. Teresa of Ávila, St. Thérèse of Lisieux, Thomas Merton, and Trappist monk Father Thomas Keating.

Modern-day mystic Reverend Cynthia Bourgeault, Ph.D., says:

Centering prayer has a very specific and substantial contribution to make to the rewiring of consciousness, precisely in the "untraditional" aspects of its methodology, namely its cultivation of a foundational capacity for attention of the heart and objectless awareness.[10]

Be aware that the benefits of an ongoing practice of contemplative prayer is not always experienced during the exercise itself. Although one can have profound experiences, even the first time, the fruits usually bloom overtime.

Much research has been done in recent years that clinically provides hard data showing how a contemplative prayer practice provides enormous benefits regardless of whether practitioners are interested in creating a closer relationship with Source/God (whatever their concept of God is) or they have had challenging life experiences and need to heal trauma and stress.

MRI scans have shown that various forms of meditation and contemplation can alter an individual's brainwaves. A 2011 Massachusetts General Hospital study found that regular meditation actually changes brain structure.[11] A regular meditative practice reduces electrical activity and blood flow in the amygdala, twin portions of the medial temporal lobe of the brain that activate emotions such as fear and anxiety, while enhancing other regions of the brain that activate compassion, focus, and clarity.[12]

It's worth noting that researchers found that different meditation and contemplation techniques stimulate different brainwave frequencies, which in turn activate and affect different parts of our neurobiology. In brief, delta waves are associated with a state the Hindus call *samadhi*—an intense and heightened state of awareness often described as union with the divine. Theta waves are associated with deep meditation and boosting the immune system. Alpha waves, provide us with wakeful relaxation and increased creativity. Beta waves reduce stress and increase confidence. Gamma waves improve decision-making and cognitive functions.

There are too many kinds of meditation practices to review and describe each one here. I recommend you do some research (the book, *Meditation for Dummies,* provides an extensive encyclopedia-like overview of most types). Try a few and stick to the one that you like best. Better yet, as I mentioned earlier, find a bona-fide teacher to guide and support you for the first few months.

In the devotee's silence, God's silence ceases.[13]
—*Paramahansa Yogananda*

This portal includes:
- Prayer.
- Raja (ashtanga) yoga.
- Breathwork.
- Vipassana.
- Zen Buddhist meditation.
- Sufi meditation.
- Visualization.

The Portal of Movement

An animating energy field surrounds and flows through us and other living things. Another important portal is movement that enables us to work with the flow of this energy. One example of this type of practice is qigong, a system of movement from China.

Qigong is an ancient practice of movement, breathing, stillness, and meditation that can accumulate and access vital energy within the body. This life force, in Chinese, is known as *qi* or *chi*. Basic qigong exercises help people quiet themselves and align their energies to the life force. Sometimes it is considered both an art and a body-technology that is a direct and powerful way to tap into the infinite source of energy. Joseph Jaworski says:

My key advice to people who want to live and work from Source and be this sort of a leader is to use at least three of the practices. I practice qigong and deeply believe that energy practices like yoga, qigong, or tai chi are significant portals to transcendental leadership.[14]

There are three components of qigong used for inducing and activating qi.

- Body/movement. The slowness of qigong movements allow for relaxation and the flow of chi energy. The deepness of the movements opens up energy channels as well as assists in the release of painful blockages. The mindful focus on the movements allows the mind to connect with the body to diminish stress and alleviate its chattering.
- Breath/sound. Specific breathing patterns and sounds activate the chi with a higher frequency and vibration and releases emotional tension.
- Mind/meditation. Positive qi and the creative power of the mind are accentuated through the practitioner's use of focus and visualization.

Qigong can have a profoundly positive affect on mental health. With it, we can learn to mentally rewire the circuitry of the brain. When the mind and the body are in energetic balance, we are able to sustain a heightened frequency of conscious awareness. Qigong is the union of qi and consciousness to awaken our connection with and access to Source.

This portal includes (among others) the pathways of:

- Hatha yoga. A system of physical postures known as *asanas*. The purpose of these postures is to provide awareness and control over the body's internal states in preparation for raja yoga (meditation).
- Athletics. A runner's high, the flow of a finely attuned team, such as we see during basketball games sometimes, or a surfer's nirvana are examples of the state focused exertion can induce.
- Dance. All types: sacred and conscious dance, Sufi dance, Indigenous trance dancing.
- Holotropic breathwork.
- Qigong and tai chi.
- Walking meditation. This is often done utilizing a labyrinth.

The Portal of Creativity

All true artists, whether they know it or not, create from a place of no-mind, from inner stillness.[15]
—*Eckhart Tolle*

Our creativity awakens in the imaginal realm, which psychologist Carl Jung called the collective unconscious. Where do we think truly original creativity comes from? Now is such an important time for the world of imagination to be utilized. We need new and innovative solutions and perspectives to create a world that works for all of us. Creatively, we might remember that not only do we live in the universe but, the universe lives within us too.

Sometimes creativity bursts out impulsively, such as when a bright idea pops into our heads seemingly from out of nowhere. Sometimes, it needs to "cook" —like when we create a stew or soup in the kitchen—simmering in the background of our daily lives for a while. We might experiment with ingredients and then give the recipe time to blend the flavors together, resulting in something new and delicious.

Most of us have tried figuring out a solution to a problem . . . thinking, thinking, thinking . . . only to go to sleep or take a nap and have the solution pop into our heads a few hours later. *Voila!*

A primary portal for Bishop Shea is creativity. She says:

Being a spiritual artist, I value the magic and meaning that comes from participating in or practicing an art form. It could be writing, playing, serving, or preparing a meal. Human activity offers an opportunity and platform for spiritual practice.

In all my practices, I do not seek simply to connect to the light and surrounding consciousness, but also to respectfully and compassionately explore the inner and outer shadows that are so much a part of who and what I am, who and what we all are. To me this is central to the cultivation of a mature mindfulness practice. This is the beginning of wisdom. Leaders attuned and in accord with, and aligned to, creative expression understand that there is a deep wisdom and knowingness that can be accessed.[16]

Encourage yourself, your colleagues, and by all means, your children, to believe that they are far more in touch and open to what is considered creative.

One of the silver linings of the global pandemic, during various lockdowns and phases of social distancing, has been people's newly discovered creativity, which goes hand in hand with one's spirituality and deep connection to the wells of ingenuity and expression.

This portal includes all forms of self-expression.

- Music and sound. Singing, drumming, playing singing bowls, chanting. Let us not underestimate the alchemical science of sound frequencies, which are powerful for healing, aligning chakras, and falling into trance-like states of mind.
- Art making. Painting, sculpting, ceramics, and drawing.
- Writing. Journaling and writing poetry.
- Theatrical performance.

You must give birth to your images. They are the future waiting to be born.[17]
—*Rainer Maria Rilke*

The Portal of Relationship

A few evenings after my first child was born, late one night, I was sitting in a chair holding his sleeping body in my arms. Without warning, I began to feel wave upon wave of the most mysterious, profound, infinite love welling up within me. It was a love far greater than any I had ever known and far greater that I had imagined possible.

Every mother knows this indescribably bonding and immensely powerful emotion. People say this is how God feels about us. My friends will tell you (as well as my sons) that I am truly a sappy, love-crazed mom.

The relationship of parents to their children may be the tip of the iceberg of the human emotion of love, but what it provides for us is the loving template of the capacity of love available in the universe. Imagine that deeply caring emotion garnered for each other, our creature and plant friends, and our living planet. This is our deepest nature: to love and be loved. To care for others. It is the foundational doctrine of all major spiritual, religious, and Indigenous wisdom traditions.

Our world is an integrated society. All of us are made up of the same "stuff" —we have an indwelling of the transcendent. None among us is undeserving of care and respect. It is paramount that our leaders truly believe this—and lead from their hearts. It is imperative that we choose to lead based on this understanding. As Jesus taught (Mark 12:31): "You must love your neighbor as yourself."[18]

In the 1980s, a group of scientists discovered that we are gifted with a mirror neuron system. Meaning that areas of our brain activate in alignment with what we see. When others act or demonstrate that they feel a certain way, our neurons recognize the movement or emotion as our own and we often are triggered, like a tuning fork, to mirror the same behavior or emotion. Mirror neurons are components of the sensory-motor system. They help infants learn hand-eye coordination and other movements swiftly. Their presence in our bodies is also helpful for social cognition.[19] When we are closely connected, our automatic nervous system joins that of our companions in harmonious rhythm.

Judi Weisbart, who does mostly nonprofit consulting, shared in an interview:

I work to have relationships that connect to the heart so that the bridge is built into the beginning construct. When I work with people I learn about their personal lives, their likes and dislikes, their concerns and accomplishments, and then we work together. I believe that all we do in life is a bridge to our soul and to the manifestation of the energy we call spirit.[20]

Compassion

How is it possible for the emphasis of power to shift from dominating and controlling, to being loving and compassionate? *Compassion*, from the Latin, means "to suffer with."

In his book, *Ethics for a New Millennium*, the Dalai Lama writes:

We can reject everything else: religion, ideology, all received wisdom. But we cannot escape the necessity of love and compassion.

This, then, is my true religion, my simple faith. In this sense, there is no need for temple or church, for mosque or synagogue, no need for complicated philosophy, doctrine, or dogma. Our own heart, our own mind, is the temple. The doctrine is compassion. Love for others and respect for their rights and dignity, no matter who or what they are: ultimately these are all we need. So long as we practice these in our daily lives, then no matter if we are learned or unlearned, whether we believe in Buddha or God, or follow some other religion or none at all, as long as we have compassion for others and conduct ourselves with restraint out of a sense of responsibility, there is no doubt we will be happy.[21]

It doesn't take much observation today to notice that too many people are suffering from a lack of compassion and empathy.

This portal overlaps with the portal of service (which we shall explore in a few pages). It is almost automatic that our compassion would call us to serve others. It is a deep commitment to compassionate serving that the transcendental leader embodies.

This portal includes:

- Community service.
- Exercises for opening of the heart.
- Romantic love and intimacy.
- Caring for our families, children, the elderly, the infirm, and animals.
- Loving and caring for the wellbeing of our planet.

The Portal of Devotion

Spiritual and religious traditions can provide a path for developing a transcendent relationship with Source, the Great Spirit, God, Brahman, Allah, and so forth. One of the Four Paths of Yoga is the practice of spiritual love and devotion that Hindus call *bhakti*. Bhakti is the surrendering devotion that allows devotees to perceive a spark of God in every person and creature they encounter, and in the entire cosmos. From this perspective, every moment is holy and love is the pervading energy.

This portal includes:

- Devotional praying, chanting, and singing.
- Pilgrimages.

- Gospel singing.
- Ceremonies at temples.
- Rituals in synagogues.
- Religious celebrations.

The Portal of Inspired Writings

I can attest that this portal is one of my favorites, along with nature and meditation. I can often feel the energetic frequency of words. The historical and significance of sound and word is a major subject in and of itself. Just know that words have an energetic signature! I love how words can be put together to describe a feeling, paint an image in my mind, or connect a spiritual truth with the mundane world. Poetry and song lyrics can make me weepy. Any of you, dear readers, who have been fortunate to be in an audience listening to poet, David Whyte, know what I mean.

Inspired writing also falls into the portal of creativity for writers. But here I am describing a reading or auditory experience. When a priest or rabbi gives a sermon and reads from scripture or a thoughtful text, it uplifts the congregants. Clearly all the gateways and pathways intersect. They join together and then drift apart in different contexts.

I've mentioned this prior, but it can't be understated that one of the most insightful sacred scriptures that has inspired countless philosophers, theologians, and political leaders such as Mahatma Gandhi, the Reverend Martin Luther King, Jr., and Nelson Mandela, who were social activists, is *The Bhagavad Gita*. Also known as the "Song of the Spirit," this 700-verse text from the second century before the common era is an abiding story combining history, revelation, and psychological and spiritual truths through parable and symbolic metaphor.

The renowned Indian guru Paramahansa Yogananda writes:

The timeless message of the Bhagavad Gita does not refer to only one historic battle, but to the cosmic conflict between good and evil: life as a series of battles between Spirit and matter, soul and body, life and death, knowledge and ignorance, health and disease, changelessness and transitoriness, self-control and temptation, discrimination and the blind sense-mind.[22]

There are many inspired writings that can uplift our minds and point toward the experience of transcendence. Some are well-known, other less so. And of course, we can only imagine what many of the ancient scrolls, symbols, and hieroglyphics could tell us if we had access to and understood them.

If this is a gateway that intrigues you and you would like to explore this further, try this: If you already love poetry or scripture or the teachings of a certain spiritual master, pick a book or reading, find a comfortable place with adequate lighting and sit quietly. Perhaps light a candle? Whether reading or listening to an audio book, respect your time and the cosmic content of the words that want to speak to you; focus, and immerse yourself – it wouldn't be unusual for you to deeply hear the words energetically come-to-life within you.

This portal includes:

- Buddhist writings about the Noble Eightfold Path of right speech, right livelihood, right thinking, right effort, right mindfulness, right action, right understanding, and right concentration.

- Inspirational literature by spiritual masters such as Thich Nhat Hanh, Paramahansa Yogananda, Sri Aurobindo, and teachers of nonduality.
- Sacred scriptures of the world's great religions, like the Torah, the Quran, and the Christian Bible.
- Biographies of the great Christian saints such as Hildegard of Bingen.
- Philosophical texts and essays.
- Evocative poetry. Try Rumi, David Whyte, John Donohue, and Mary Oliver.
- Channeled texts that teach love and nonduality, such as *A Course in Miracles*.

The Portal of Service

Another gateway is the path through selfless service. Considered one of the five pillars of the Islamic spiritual tradition, this is known as *zakat*. The gateway of selfless service is also found in the Hindu tradition, where it is called *karma*. In Buddhism, right action, right livelihood, and right effort—from the Noble Eightfold Path, are invoked by service. Jesus establishes the Golden Rule in the Sermon on the Mount when he says: "Do unto others as you would have them do unto you" (Leviticus 19:18).

We heard numerous stories during the global pandemic of nurses, doctors, and all other manner of healing professionals and first responders, including supermarket checkout clerks, putting themselves at risk of contagion to serve others in their time of need.

This portal includes:

- Healing work.
- Medical personnel.
- Teachers.
- Community social workers.
- Caretakers for the elderly, for the mentally, emotionally, and physically disabled, and for any and all disenfranchised people.
- Firefighters and paramedics.
- Elected officials (governance).
- Volunteers.
- Farm workers and food-processing plant workers.

Love cannot remain by itself—it has no meaning. Love has to be put into action. And that action is service.
—*Mother Teresa*

The Portal of Knowing

The portal of knowing is characterized by studying the vastness of cosmology or anything that helps us understand reality and develop our spiritual awareness.

Roger Tempest and Paris Ackrill brought the following example to my attention during their interview with me:

There was enormous synchronicity around the incorporation of sacred geometry and geomancy into the Avalon buildings at Broughton Hall. Originally, some postcards were given to us with Sacred Geometry and the idea found a strong foothold in Paris' awareness. The interior designer also happened to see the cards and quickly received clarity on how to incorporate it. It was only afterwards, that we discovered that the Hall had been built in a Fibonacci year (1089).[23]

In the past, I attended lectures given by mathematician and evolutionary cosmologist Brian Swimme, Ph.D., in which he described the unfolding evolution of our planet and I was overcome with a sensation of deeply knowing my connection, meaning, and place in the world. I felt that I had a reason for being on this planet at this time in history.

In Hinduism, the path of wisdom and learning is known as *jnana.*

In my interview with Roger Walsh, M.D., Ph.D., University of California Medical School, author and teacher in transpersonal psychology, he shared that he is particularly drawn to jnana yoga as one of his primary portals, as it is cerebral in nature. Here is an insight from him regarding elements of transpersonal psychology in the context of the portal of knowing.

Advance contemplatives have demonstrated numerous psychological capacities that formerly were thought impossible. When you're open to capacities and potentials that we might be able to develop, which most of us haven't even thought of, it revises our mindset and view of human nature. Knowing and sensing provide an expanded view of human potentials and capacities that—whether dreamed or defined—heighten perceptual sensitivities and deepen skills. We now have, for the first time in human history, the world's reservoir or library of such transpersonal practices and accompanying psychologies and philosophies available to us. We now know that these capacities are more than just capacities. Virtues can be cultivated and we have ways to do so. We now have a transpersonal framework for introducing the possibility of accessing levels of knowledge, insight, wisdom, and guidance that before might not make much sense whatsoever to people. These portals are access points to transcendental realms."[24]

Fundamentally, wisdom is a state of human consciousness characterized by a relaxed, yet alert awareness, compassionate emotional intelligence, diminished internal, mental dialogue, and the capacity to engage with everyday reality, without the artifice of both personal and collective mental and emotional triggers. These capacities for knowing and wisdom is most often grokked and accessed through self-inquiry, thoughtful study, and spiritual practice.

This portal includes:

- Consciousness studies.
- Sacred geometry.
- Cosmology.
- The yogic path of jnana.
- Psychology, in particular transpersonal psychology.
- Quantum physics.

The Portal of Indigenous Wisdom

In holistic physicist F. David Peat's book *Blackfoot Physics*, he compares and reveals the similarities between ancient and Indigenous shamanic teachings from around the world to insights emerging from modern science. One such concept is the notion that there is no separation between anything—that wholeness and connection exists within all life and matter in the universe. Matter, humankind, and spirit are one. Our perceptions can be shifted, which in turn can reframe what we think is our reality in order to allow more expanded ways of seeing, feeling, perceiving, and knowing.

Jim Garrison, Ph.D., muses:

> *When you allow your perceptions to be altered, you can begin to grant in data consistent with your new perceptions and exclude other data not consistent with your current perceptions. That's why all the major mystics and mystical practitioners, such as Don Juan and Carlos Castaneda, say the most important thing is your perception—because your perception governs everything. So, in my experience, shifting your perception is definitively a key to allowing the transcendence in.*[25]

One of the portals valued by Stephan Rechtschaffen M.D., is plant medicine. He says:

> *Nature has given us many plant medicines, which allow us to easily transverse that place between consciousness and inner nature. The experience is different than let's say meditation, but it's one of the portals that's immediately available and*

doesn't require years of practice. So, for me, there's plant medicine and meditation. Especially meditation with anything that relates to nature. I would say they are my prime entry points.[26]

Indigenous wisdom has held centuries-old models of leadership and stewardship of our planet and its wellbeing. And to this day, it holds intergenerational and holistic knowledge that much of humanity has, sadly, discarded in modern times.

The portal of Indigenous wisdom helps us experience how we as living beings are in relationship with everything else and in a constant state of evolving.

The portal of Indigenous wisdom includes:

- Shamanic vision quests.
- Psychedelic plant medicines, like ayahuasca and peyote.
- Indigenous rituals and ceremonies, including the Medicine Wheel or the Pachakuti Mesa.
- Hypnotic drumming and dancing.
- Totem guardians, spirit animals, and shape-shifting.

The Portal of Yoga

I have separated out four individual elements of the path of yoga and incorporated them into previous portals, where they definitely belong. However, I must reiterate them here as the impact of the science and practice of yoga on us as transcendent leaders cannot be underestimated. Yoga has been practiced since ancient times, providing benefits ranging from the physical to the mental to the emotional to the spiritual to enlightenment and full *awakening*.

In addition, let me stress that the yoga I am addressing is not the version of yoga taught in gyms as an athletic exercise program consisting of postures for toning and strengthening the physical body. My intent is to describe eternal yoga (meaning union) very briefly, as it was originally taught in the East, as a practice and process for spiritual unfolding and becoming harmoniously balanced. This is a portal and practice that, I feel, requires a thoughtful, sincere, and deep commitment. Human in union with Source.

Although I've addressed the four paths somewhat already, to reiterate, they are:

- Jnana yoga—*union* of all existence: the path of wisdom and knowing. I placed jnana yoga in the portal of knowing; however, it *also* belongs in the portal of meditation and contemplative practices because it incorporates *deep* meditative inquiry.

- Raja yoga—*union* between one's lower self and higher self: the path of meditation and mysticism. I placed raja yoga in the portal of meditation and contemplative practices because its primary path is the gateway of deep meditation leading to realization and transcendence.

- Bhakti yoga—*union* between oneself and Source: the path of devotion and love. I placed bhakti yoga in the portal of devotion because its primary gateway is the heartfelt love and deep dedication to the Divine.

- Karma yoga—*union* between the individual and others: the path of selfless action. I placed karma yoga in the portal of service, yet it also belongs in the portal of relationship, because through karma yoga we imbue ourselves with humility and let go of our egos through serving others. And not just those we are close to, such as our family members and friends, but also our community, organizations, and planet. I suppose we could also include this in the portal of nature, if we are to embrace service to our beloved planet and Gaia, yes?

Alignment with Transcendence Is an Imperative of Our Era

Transcendental leadership differs from other models of leadership because its foundation is in the transcendental leader's realization that we are *all* part of the orderly universe, and that intrinsic within ourselves is the essence of all—Source. They recognize Source in their own being. Such leaders embrace *all* life.

As a leader, desiring to be a transcendent leader, your commitment to a consistent practice will provide you with heightened awareness, which will positively influence everything you do in your life and all the people you lead and the causes you serve. I believe accessing states of transcendence with your portals is an essential tool for the transcendental leader.

We are in the midst of a very serious, yet necessary shifting of the consciousness of *everyone* on the planet. In this transitional period, we are being given the opportunity to press the refresh button. We are at a critical choice-point because of the intersection of multiple simultaneous crises. The global family is experiencing all manner of breakdown and tragedy, ranging from the viral outbreaks and climate change to social oppression and economic disparity and uncertainty.

Those of us who are in positions of influence must *take responsibility for our being* and begin aligning ourselves with the deep knowing and wisdom that is accessible to each of us, intrinsically available, and which is our cosmic heritage. How can it not be? If the God-spark is what created the cosmos, how can it not be within us as well? It's therefore imperative to reach towards the possibility—the silver lining of hope—that we will change our old, collective blind-leading-the-blind behaviors and begin to unite for the sake of each other and future generations. The moment of choice is *now*.

In an interview with Bishop Heather Shea, she shared her ability to be open to various portals of transcendence.

My entire life I have walked between multiple dimensions with nonphysical, multidimensional spirits, and quantum realms being real and accessible to me. Our current culture does not have a great term for it so I use mystic *or* sage. *I believe we all have access and leverage it in our own ways. It can be that moment when we are praying. We may feel it when reading legendary transcendental authors like Emerson, Thoreau, or Whitman. Or, hearing, playing, or dancing to our favorite music—when we know we are in flow and connected to a larger energy. It is the sound of leaves rustling or a babbling brook flowing by. Information can just arrive in our mind or we ask for guidance or prepare ourselves through work or contemplation for divine intervention or a personal insight. I also attend classes, work with spiritual coaches, study great literature, take time with nature, engage in the arts, have an active altar, engage daily with the Divine, access goddesses, archetypal energies, look to spirit guides and animals, and say my prayers.*

Developing one's ability to connect with divine knowledge is a skill and capacity that strengthens and becomes more attuned with practice over time. Spiritual practices provide a portal to cultivate the personal abilities and inner capacities to be able to manifest new realities and work with others in collaboration with this living planet and cosmos, a cocreative partnership to explore and experiment our way to a new sustainable future.[27]

Anyone aspiring to develop and accelerate their own self-awareness and thereby to *transcend* to the stage of transcendental leadership will appreciate the results of practicing one or several of these portals.

As mentioned before, people may take different paths to open to the transcendent experience within themselves: the path to inner awareness, Source realization, or awakening, has many names. Some individuals commit to only one practice because it resonates powerfully for them. Others choose several practices and use a combination of portals to deepen their connection and alignment. For example, in my interview with Jim Garrison, I asked him about his portals and he said:

My portal-practices have been pretty consistent over forty years. I'm a devotee of yoga; and for about thirty years, I ran the equivalent of about a marathon every week, not all at once, but over the course of seven days; and I try to swim a lot. Although yoga and physical movement have been very important, I also have a consistent and deep meditative practice. If you do that on a daily basis, it doesn't save you from mistakes or stress, but it helps to illuminate your pathway in very subtle ways that you appreciate more and more over time.[28]

Like Shea and Garrison, and many of the other leaders I interviewed, it has always seemed prudent to me to embrace two or three practices myself and use the other portals, especially those that I enjoy and resonate with, as opportunities to pursue my evolution in consciousness, spiritual awareness, emotional growth, and development in transcendental leadership. For me, during the time of sequestering and social isolation from the pandemic, I stepped up my meditation practice, ate primarily vegetarian and organic foods, read books, and listened to audio recordings filled with wisdom on how to raise my vibrational frequency and achieve flow and synchronicity. I did more body/energy work and spent *lots* more time in solitude, silence, and nature. My meditations became deeper, as a result, and I found myself, as Ralph Waldo Emerson might have said, *feeling the embrace of nature and insight.*

I have touched upon how profound and important writing this book has been for me, because writing about alignment to

Source *activates* and *calls* Source into my being like a radio dial or a tuning fork. Mind you, Source/God is always and already present anyway. But when I realize and am aware of it in myself—when I feel, sense, and silently *hear* Source within me—then I see "It" reflected in the beauty of nature, others, all life forms, and the entire cosmos.

In this vein, I take the time to sit in the grass, close my eyes to meditate, and feel the warm breeze and sunlight of a warm summer day on my face. Today, I can hear the soft tinkling of chimes, the splashing of cascading water from the outdoor fountain behind me, an occasional toot from a train in the distance, and the melodious harmony of softly pealing bells from numerous ancient medieval churches scattered throughout the rural country villages (I wrote this portion of the book while I was still living above stunning Lake Orta in northern Italy). I invite Source, become quiet, suspend and surrender any thoughts, and embrace the stillness.

Our world is so extraordinary. It's wonderful when leaders make the choice to humbly self-realize their connection and unity with Source, everyone, and everything. As influencers, they foster others to have similar experiences and realizations.

REFLECTION EXERCISE

Here are a few questions to reflect upon in order to discern the portals and practices that most thoroughly align and resonate with your unique you.

Firstly, I suggest you take as much time as necessary to deeply reflect upon and inquire within yourself as to what your best portals may be. If you are a novice at this kind of thing, it may take a bit longer than if you are already familiar with one or more of these portals. But you can trust your instincts on this as much as anyone else can. Your heart holds the answer.

I wouldn't be surprised if you have already experienced many aha moments in the past—though perhaps not having previously realized that meditative and thoughtful hiking in the mountains could be considered a portal to awakening. Most people have experienced moments of transcendence and peak/peek/pique epiphanies at some point in their lives!

Bottom line, where are *you* discovering *your* doorways to peak/peek/pique states of transcendence? Find your access points and get cooking. States of flow, greater awareness, and synchronistic moments of grace will align with you as you lead from your being—aligned with Source, truth, and the wisdom of the cosmos.

These questions will help you be certain of your choices. Ask:

- How do I personally define Source/God/the Divine?
- In which activities do I lose track of time?
- How would I personally describe a transcendent or peak experience?
- In what kinds of situations have I distinctly heard an inner voice of wisdom?
- In what ways have I felt hunches or intuitively known something?
- What were the circumstances where I have had an aha moment?

- Reminiscing on my experiences of the portals described in Chapter 4, in doing which two or three practices or activities have I found moments of bliss and deep joy?

Although a sudden and unexpected numinous illumination can occur, seemingly out of the blue, it is uncommon for those who have not been consistently aligning with and tuning their inner channels for connecting with Source. Creating within yourself a clear ability to intuitively hear, sense, feel, and be open to Source requires a regular practice.

Don't be confused or disappointed if your new practice, at first, doesn't provide the *connection* to Source you expect or hope for. Think of yourself as taking baby steps. Like they say, you can't run before you learn to walk. Your system has to acclimate and evolve. Please simply trust you are on the right path if you are doing something every day to connect.

To paraphrase a line from the writing of the legendary Chinese sage Lao Tzu: If you want to awaken humanity, then you must first awaken yourself. The greatest gift you have to give is that of your own transformation.

V

TRANSCENDENTAL LEADERSHIP IN ACTION TODAY

I believe each one of us is born with a destiny and the whole journey of life is to discover what that destiny is. The key principle of following your destiny and manifesting what it is that Source is making available to you is that you must manifest this as Source desires, not as you desire.
—Joseph Jaworski, cofounder and chairman of Generon International

To begin, let me share a story of a transcendental leader I feel blessed to call a good friend. This story is somewhat indicative of how an individual can come to *know* their calling, purpose, and passion—or destiny as Joseph Jaworski says in the quote above. Your destiny, calling, purpose, I have learned through personal research, often begins to surface as a youngster even if it is forgotten for many years or the impetus to pursue a particular path is not yet understood or undertaken.

In this case, it begins with a question that I have asked myself and have often asked the many teachers and leaders that I have met. My question is: "Do you remember an instance when you were a young boy or girl, that something happened in your life, that may have generated, or seeded your compelling calling or purpose in life?"

In October 2017, I was fortunate to encounter a brand-new retreat center located in the spectacular Lakes Region of northern Italy. Situated on a mountain hillside overlooking the stunning, yet serene Lago d'Orta is the extraordinary Mandali Retreat Center. It had been opened for about six months when I first came to visit. As luck would have it, one of the Dutch owners, Wildrik Timmerman, was there at the same time. Staff shared with me that I should meet him while he was there, and simultaneously, the management was telling Wildrik that he should meet the woman visiting from California because at the time I worked at a retreat center in Santa Barbara, California.

Never underestimate the winds of destiny or the ways the field of coherence brings complementary people together! Synchronistically, Wildrik and I were both departing for Milan Malpensa Airport the next day, so he offered me a ride. In this way, we would have a quiet hour together to get acquainted.

I was very curious and interested in the story behind how he and his business partner, Wouter Tavecchio, after building a successful organization in the music festival business in Amsterdam, had come to completely switch gears, become spiritually transformed, and undertake a mission to build a world-class retreat center.

Eventually, I asked my definitively curious question: "Do you remember anything as a young boy that may have planted the seed and generated your purpose to serve in the spiritual transformation of humanity?"

Wildrik immediately said no, but then quickly paused to muse. "Wait a minute," he said. I witnessed a shift in his being, a transformation of his countenance, and could see him going back into his childhood memory bank. He took a deep, thoughtful breath and shared what was clearly a recollection of an emotional experience. "I had completely forgotten about this until just now, at least in the context," he said, "however, when I was about six years old, I went to a Catholic school. My parents didn't embrace the doctrine, they just felt I would get a good education. I didn't believe in God either."

Wildrik paused again in his reflection and, I think, there was a bit of awe and wonder at the aha realization bubbling to the surface of his mind. He continued, "There was a little girl in my class and, one day, the teacher told us that she was seriously ill and was going to die. I went home and prayed that night to a God I didn't believe in, asking for her to live and telling God that I would believe in Him if He would let her live . . . and she lived."

I can tell you (with Wildrik's permission) that while we were in the car zipping down the mountainside, this masculine, young, handsome, and friendly, successful man in his early forties had gentle tears slowly rolling down his cheeks. Without thinking, I put a comforting hand on his shoulder and felt the energetic poignancy of his realization. In a flash, two strangers shared a spiritual coherence and connection, something that cannot be orchestrated or strategized. He then explained that this experience might have been the first push that set the train of his spiritual path in motion.

Mandali Retreat Center came from a *place* of Wildrik and Wouter *truly wanting to give for the pure joy of giving.*

We live in a time of many great teachers and leaders—and we are learning from each other, too, as we collectively wake up. Learning from the bottom up as well as from the top down. I believe that there are omnipresent forces everywhere around the globe. Some people with quiet voices of great clarity are leading today. Some we may be familiar with; however, most we are not. There are many on the leading-edge of transformation that are less known, yet they are defying the odds in supplanting the narrative of shareholder supremacy with a new narrative of mutual wellbeing for the employee, the customer, and humanity in general through bravely championing regenerative choices and expressing thoughtful consideration for people, animals and our planet. These are individuals who have a conscious, purposeful desire, no matter the odds, to serve others and to lead humanity to a more just, loving, peaceful, and healthy life experience.

How This Book Came Together

Throughout this book we have seen how the notion of transcendental leadership is grounded in being beyond ego, personality, and the mind. Leaders displaying this kind of leadership exercise self-awareness and presence-eliciting traits, among others, of authenticity, humility, and openness. They regularly utilize practices and portals to engender states of transcendent awareness that then inform and provide them with alignment to the holographic cosmic field of universal wisdom. In addition, their evolution into a higher state of consciousness involves developing a transcendent sense of self, which also gives them the capacity to handle more complex perspectives as leaders.

In this chapter, I'll be sharing with you examples of transcendental leadership in action today. I want to provide you, my reader, with first-hand accounts from individuals exemplifying the traits we discussed in Chapter 3 and their insights on the portals they utilize, from Chapter 4, to align themselves with Source in order to inform and guide their leadership.

We'll start with those primary dimensions from Chapter 3 from which the traits and attributes, such as humility, authenticity, deep listening, the capacity to suspend judgment, come from. In their own words, I will allow them to describe how they:

- Tap into universal wisdom.
- Practice awareness and presence.
- Contribute to serving the whole.

And we'll learn from some of these leaders about the various portals and practices they utilize regularly to prompt awakening and experience transcendence, which we reviewed in Chapter 4.

Many individuals are leading from a place of transcendence aligned with Source. Every day, they are tapping into universal wisdom, practicing awareness and presence, and contributing to the whole of humanity and the Earth. Although I have chosen only a few to showcase here, all the people in this category lead wisely in their own communities and are making a significant difference across the spectrum of social activism, civil rights, and visionary leadership practices, forwarding an authentic and new modality to leading and shifting age-old, mostly patriarchal worldviews.

Some of these individuals I've been honored to meet, some I have been able to interview, and some I researched. For those that I was fortunate to interview, I created a questionnaire that, I hoped, would provide a generative starting point for them to share their experiences and thoughts about transcendental leadership, such as their ideas on the traits of transcendental leadership and details about the portals and practices they personally utilized to align themselves with Source/God/the field of universal wisdom. They answered the call and generously included their own stories and anecdotes to aid this project.

There were several ways I gathered data for this book (and for my original thesis).

1. Background research. I read many books, articles, reports of peer-reviewed research studies, video transcripts, and scriptures, listened to audios, and watched videos and then formed an outline of general themes that I postulated

would be significant to leaders. Always asking and listening for guidance from Source.

2. I developed a questionnaire/survey that was distributed to almost thirty leaders. Twenty-five individuals responded to it. I viewed this as a vehicle for nudging an essay-style, stream-of-consciousness response from the respondents that would include anecdotes and examples of transcendental experiences informing their leadership behavior and thinking. I drew some of these individuals from several groups I'm involved with, such as the Institute of Noetic Sciences, the Conscious Leadership Guild, the Evolutionary Leaders Circle, the Source of Synergy Foundation, and the Women's Executive Network, as well as reaching out to the owners and founders of several international retreat centers, graduate university professors and administrators, and global thought leaders and authors dedicated to the transformation and upliftment of humanity.

3. Interviews were conducted remotely on a video platform. I recorded our conversation, and then, in reviewing the transcript, would attempt to ascertain and highlight their thoughts experiences, stories and opinions. Let me say again how enormously grateful I am to these kind-hearted, supportive individuals wanting to start an open dialogue and contribute to a new narrative of leadership.

For the sake of brevity and in cases where different people offered similar, overlapping insights, some of the remarks have been edited.

The Transcendental Leadership Questionnaire

Here are some of the questions I asked in my survey and interviews. You may want to reflect upon them yourself, either as you read them now or after reading the chapter.

1. What might be your notion of transcendental leadership? And how does the larger construct of this idea resonate with you?

2. How do you bridge your business, organizational, and relationship decisions with your spiritual/conscious awareness?

3. Drawing from the categories below, do you have one or more main spiritual portals/practices that you use to access higher levels of consciousness and inner wisdom, and which inform your leadership? Please expand on your experiences of:

   • Nature.
   • Meditation and contemplation.
   • Movement.
   • Creativity.
   • Relationship.
   • Devotion.
   • Inspired writings.
   • Service.
   • Knowing.

- Indigenous wisdom.
- Yoga.

4. In what ways do you think these practices (portals) evoke, engage, and provide universal wisdom and awareness? Can you provide any examples in your own experience?

5. Grouped by three primary dimensions—universal wisdom, awareness and presence, and service to the whole—in your opinion, what traits and attributes characterize a transcendental leader? And why? What do you think are your best traits?

6. In what ways do you utilize ritual in your capacity as a leader? Can you share examples and your thoughts on how or why you utilize them?

Now, in no particular order, let's hear directly from leaders on the path of transcendence.

Selected Voices from the Surveys and Interviews

Jim Garrison, Ph.D., President, Ubiquity University and Founder, Humanity Rising (California and the Netherlands)

"Leading from a place of transcendence is, in its essence, allowing transcendence to inform the imminent, and for the imminent to inform the transcendent—so that the inner and the outer, the spiritual and the activistic, the sacred and the profane are united in a way that enables a person to hold a spiritual awareness while they're leading. For example, as in my case, taking political action. I would also say that transcendental leadership is at the heart of sacred activism.

"Consistent practice is how you allow the transcendent into the imminent. My parents were missionaries in Asia, and when I was five years old, wandering around one morning I saw a monk in meditation at a Buddhist temple. He was sitting so still that I became intrigued and realized that he was truly somewhere else—in a very, very deep place. Witnessing him in a transcendent state, for me as a little boy, was so remarkable that it is imprinted on my consciousness to the present day. It may have been the most important experience of my entire life, informing who I am.

"Understanding that the numinous was real and intuitively understanding that the Buddhists were not going to go to hell because they weren't Christians set up an amazing dialectic between me and the prevailing religious culture. Because the experience with the Buddhist monk had been so indelible—it didn't go away—it reoriented my ontology and opened me up to other experiences that in any other circumstance wouldn't have had any effect.

"When I was about an eight or nine, I was listening to a missionary tell stories of being in China and Tibet, where my parents were wanting to go. And he said, 'They keep mumbling these words all the time,' so I asked him, 'What are the words they're mumbling?'

"He said, '*Om mani padme hum, om mani padme hum,*' and as soon as he said those words, that mantra, the mantra kind of sailed across the room and hit me right between the eyes! I've been repeating it ever since. It's my mantra. At the time, I didn't understand what a mantra was any more than I understood what meditation was."

"Rituals: It's good at the beginning of a meeting to check in, 'How are you feeling that day?' Some people may think, 'Oh, let's get to the agenda, we don't have time for this,' but that's when the energetic quality of human-to-human biochemistry actually works out. Being in the presence of another person changes your chemistry. Literally when a strong person walks into the room, chemical changes happen to people. You've got to be aware that that's true. And because that's true, you can access it. Then you become more aware of the subtleties of the energetics in a room.

"The energetics in a room or on a zoom call are very important. It's every person, every time of day, everywhere. That's because feng shui matters. Your energetic qualities are different in a pyramid than in a square room than in a round room.

"One of the tragedies of modernity is thinking we can dispense with ritual and live in a completely rational world. But that's not the way human beings are constructed. You know, every day on our podcast, 'Humanity Rising,' we do a one-minute-long heart coherence meditation. And I can't tell you how many people have written me saying that it is so important. It just takes ninety seconds and everybody kind of drops in. Once you've dropped in, your heart is open and your body chemistry has been changed.

"This is not fluffy stuff. When transcendence and imminence meet, there are biochemical changes in the body that can be actually measured. For example, when you do a heart coherence meditation, something like 1,400 changes occur in your heart brain, and body chemistry as a result. And it takes under three minutes.

"Ritual is not an abstraction. Ritual is an incarnation of transcendence into the imminent world."

Bishop Heather Shea, CEO and Spiritual Director, United Palace of Spiritual Arts (New York)

"A transcendental leader to me is one who is at home being with themself and integrated with and evoking universal consciousness. Transcendental leadership understands that the human person's highest motivator is deeply spiritual in nature.

"Transcendental leadership is grounded in a profound respect for the dignity of the individual human person and a deep reverence for the entirety of society and creation. Transcendental leaders are motivated by this love, respect, and reverence.

"Transcendental leadership springs from an all-encompassing personal ethical core and moral vision. They articulate a collective vision that promises to propel the people in and around their organizations to higher levels of moral living, ethical and social achievement, and collective evolution. It is also about individual and collective healing, health, growth, development, evolution, and transformation. As such, it is grounded in the commitment to realize the future human person and the potential human society.

"Transcendental leadership arises from a deep and healthy integration of the heart and mind, of the feminine and the masculine, the individual and the collective, the progressive and the conservative; in short, it is a leadership style that seeks integration and transcendence.

"My years of leadership development in running prestigious global organizations, gives me the traditional confidence, competence, and endurance to take on the leadership challenges and opportunities this position offers me. I am an ordained bishop with a background in finance, law, marketing, and facilities management. And even show business. Much of my career was also spent in talent development. A leader is not a leader without followers. Recruiting, retaining, rewarding, and developing talent is a dedicated focus of mine. During the time of the covid-19 pandemic, when most all theaters were closed and staff furloughed, we stayed open, providing our staff with full benefits and pay. It was a time for great growth, development, and success for the organization because of a culture committed to everyone in it and the community we serve.

"Early on, I recognized that the scope and breadth of my position required divine intervention and assistance. It is indeed a daily practice for me to access the great knowing to manifest change and motion in this dimension. I know at a fundamental level what needs to be done. By praying or channeling or asking, or whatever you want to call it, I asked the universe to solve or resolve my biggest and some of my smaller challenges. Remarkable how the wildest dreams do come true."

"A transcendental leader is one who follows a moral compass. Period. They know how to discern right from wrong. They do the right thing, no matter how difficult it may seem at the time. This includes for yourself, your staff, your family, and people within the organization, when handling the finances and all business-related decisions and integrations.

"A transcendental leader asks and listens to the guidance provided by divine sources, which can also be the universal energy evoking our inner capacities and strengthening our actions and abilities.

"This leader knows that they are living in a dimension within multiple dimensions and in unity with all others. There is no us or them. The yin and yang, divine feminine and divine masculine, are both required to thrive within every leader. So that's how I look at what I can do. I can do a balance sheet. I can make sure that people are paid well. I mean, that's hard by the way, doing balance sheets and legal paperwork, and making sure people are paid during a pandemic and that the people are healthy and that you're best in class and you're following all the rules. That's all very hard.

"While I use my guides and intuition constantly, in this environment—and this is important, I think, for leaders to know—it's possible to get woo-wooed away. 'Oh, I feel this' and 'Oh, I believe that.' That's all very well, regardless of where you're pulling it from. However, in this day and age, it's critical also to know what the best legal and pragmatic leadership practices are. What's your strategy? What are your goals? What are your tactics? What are the finances? What are the implications? What's your projection? Does this come before Spirit? Which one's more important? It's how you work them together so that people are comfortable—and because that takes you to the next level.

"You balance the hard skills with an attunement to spiritual realms providing guidance."

Stephan Rechtschaffen, M.D., Founder, Omega Institute for Holistic Studies (New York), Blue Spirit Costa Rica, and the Nosara Longevity Center and Author (Costa Rica)

"My sense of transcendent leadership is that it's for the larger *sense of the whole.* As the world has evolved, there's more focus on the 'I' rather than the 'we.' And we've seen that there's more focus on the 'mind' rather than the 'feeling sense' or the 'emotional body,' and we live in a state of imbalance as a result of it.

"That's the picture of the *whole,* and whenever I create something in a project or otherwise, I focus on the whole, bringing it all together as one, and *finding what unites all of the different aspects.*

"I feel leadership is not being at the top and having everybody doing things for you. I'm part of the team here at Blue Spirit Costa Rica. I just happen to hold a certain position, it's not better or worse. I enjoy what I do and I really honor the people who work with me, and it's been incredibly fruitful here because I see people in our leadership blossoming because they haven't worked in a situation like this before, where their opinions are listened to. They matter; everybody gets a voice. So that, to me, is what we need to be looking at—rather than a top-down hierarchy, we have to make sure that the horizontal is as important as the vertical. Then you have a *whole* balance.

"Ritual: When people gather, they're often in very different rhythms. I think doing a silent practice to bring everybody into rhythm is valuable. To me, the purpose of the beginning of the meeting is to bring everybody into rhythm together, and you can do that in many ways. You can do that with a silence, you can do that with a led meditation, you can do that with playing some music or other rituals that can be done. And I think it really serves the group because you start to bring everybody into a cohesive, rhythmic pattern where then the conversation flows.

"To me, it's like doing meditation without effort. While a meeting should have agreement and potentially have certain things that get decided, in our situation at Blue Spirit, we can say: 'Let's just be here together and out of our being together, we'll look at the issues that are here and we'll come to agreement about it.' And so that's what I enjoy now more. Certainly, it's an opportunity I have here that I didn't have in larger organizations.

"Portals: Being in Costa Rica, nature is critical. And one of the things about being in nature is how it changes your rhythm. Nature is happening at a very different rhythm than the modern world. And this allows one to slow down and *simply be with things*. As soon as you do that, you start to *feel* more than just think. So, partly to me, the portal is the potential to slow stuff down and come into rhythm with one's understanding.

"How can I help people reconnect to what their true nature is? I'm open to helping people find what's most directly connected to their intrinsic beauty. We all want to find that, that's the journey. And the key is not to get lost in that journey by looking at a goal of money, success, all of those western accolades.

"We have to get to the *we*, and so transcendent leadership has to be beyond the me. We live as a community, but then we think we're different and separate than everybody else who's living around us. Also, we treat nature as an object, yet the demise that's happening to nature is the demise that's happening to the health of the human population and the planet.

"Anybody who's in a position of leadership who isn't seeing the *whole* circle of life around them, who isn't paying attention to what's happening to the planet, to the animals, to the nature around them is not really, to me deserving of the term leader.

"I remember hiking over mountain passes with my dear friend Roshi Joan Halifax in northern Nepal, going from one small village to the next, providing medical care. One day, we came to the cave where the great Hindu saint Sai Baba had done long-term meditations. We're sitting there in meditation, and I had the experience of looking out over the mountains and down into the valley to the next mountain in the Himalayas. And I realized in that moment that Sai Baba had sat there many, many years before me, and the view that I had was no different than the view he had before, it had not changed. And by him sitting and just being in that present state, he changed the world because of the deepening that took place in his being; that's how wisdom spreads into the world in a very profound way.

"We tend to think that doing is what changes things—and the lesson is: It's not the doing but *being* where we change things in an important way. We don't take enough time to drop into *being*, so again, it's the *doing and the being*, we're human doings instead of human beings. How do we drop into our *being* nature? *That's where the wisdom is.*"

Jude Currivan, Ph.D., Cosmologist, Author, and Cofounder of WholeWorld View (United Kingdom)

"A few years ago, I was in Santa Barbara, California, with my dear friend the visionary Barbara Marx Hubbard. We'd been hosted, as part of a small gathering, to have an inquiring dialogue together. Afterward, someone who'd heard us speak, approached us and kindly said, 'You're my role models.' She then paused before adding, 'No, you're my *soul* models.'

"When I was invited to contribute my sense of transcendental leadership here, those words returned, as I feel they're the epitome of what transcendental leadership embodies as certainly it did for Barbara, and as I aspire to living it in my own life.

"The opportunity to tread such inner-to-outer journeys, while unique to everyone is also, it seems to me, common to our human heritage and offers numerous routes up the same mountain. My own path has increasingly valued intuitive insights and synchronicities as way showers and with the presence of joy, love, and gratitude as my cherished companions along the way.

"Indeed, learning from nature's wisdom, perceiving our planetary home as our primary mother, and healing our relationship with her is, for me, the most fundamental call to transcendental leadership, inviting us to level up equality and justice and, so, to light up the future flourishing of ourselves, Gaia, and all her other children.

"Integration of the trinity of the unity of a wholistic worldview and (r)evolutionary purpose and the distributed intelligence of unity in diversity stimulates transformational change from the inside out. It's transcendental leadership, that then balances and complements the best practices of the predominantly masculine behaviors of the past with feminine attributes in an emergent integration.

"Such transcendental leadership is vital if we're to collectively cocreate the now and the future we want for ourselves, our children and our planetary home. And heeding the (r)evolutionary call to link up and lift up, level up and light up, invites us all to come together in a global movement of hope in action."

Joseph Jaworski, Cofounder and Chairman, Generon International and Founder and Chairman, Global Leadership Initiative (Texas)

"A transcendental leader has the capacity to consistently manifest new realities. To me, that is the hallmark. And this is the leader who lives and works from Source. Pure and simple.

"My key advice to people who want to live and work from Source and be this sort of a leader is to use at least three of the practices. The first would be nature as a portal to transmit leadership. I've spent the last thirty or forty years focusing on that and taking people out in nature for long solos. Even being in nature for a two-hour walk is a way to tap into Source, or just being outdoors under a tree for thirty minutes a day is a way to do it.

"When I was working in Amsterdam with Shell, there's a beautiful park near the office in the Hague. I would consistently pause meetings and we would take solo or paired walks during our breaks, and consistently, people would come back with new ideas and deeper commitments on something that they were proposing.

Another practice is qigong. I deeply believe that energy and movement practices like yoga, qigong, or tai chi are significant portals to transcendental leadership. And another one, of course, is contemplative practices and meditation. But the key to all of it is being disciplined; not to the point where it is a have-to and you dread doing it, but consistently using these disciplines as a portal. Consistency is important because transcendence is a capacity that is built over time.

"For me, the way that being informed by Source works is that you actually have a dialogue with Source. For example, you are seeking the answer to a problem or a situation, such as an organizational or societal issue; and you ask for the guidance. Then, you remain open for the answer from Source until an answer is provided. At that point, you must act on that answer. And when you do act, that's the ticket for the next day's answer, so to speak.

"The unmanifest is hidden. It's the Implicate Order that physicist David Bohm talks about. Sometimes I call it the *plane of possibility.* This information arises within you.

As you become open for the answer to arise, observe. Then, just before going to the deeper place of knowing, surrender and let go. And just before you act in an instant is letting come (allowing).

"The whole point of the additional two coordinates is the whole concept of surrendering false knowledge, surrendering all of your prior knowledge so that pure information from Source can arrive. This can be very hard.

"Letting go to let come can be quite challenging. It's imperative that we consistently practice alignment to Source within the portals. Our capacity to raise our frequency helps cleanse the filters that we have, the mindsets and views that we hold; and provides us with an energetic ability to attract the answers and solutions we are seeking, like a tuning fork. That's part of the letting go to let come. There's the heart and mind and soul of the individual's commitment to resolving the particular issue.

"To me, commitment is paramount in cleansing the filters. It's about intention and pure intention. And the commitment to let go of your ego, which is not in service of the answer that you're seeking, so you may instead be committed to serving the whole.

"When you are committed to manifesting important new realities, it can be a hard decision to take that journey; it's intimately akin to the hero's journey that mythologist Joseph Campbell talks about. And many times, you go down this road of trials, or in fact, all times it's archetypal when you're manifesting a new reality. You're going to encounter a lot of resistance, particularly if it's a brand-new reality, and that's the road of trials that you're going to go through. That is the test of how committed you are. Part of the interior condition that enables us to go down the road of trials, trudge through the dark night of the soul, and persevere is the feeling that you have stepped into your own destiny.

"I believe each one of us is born with a destiny and the whole journey of life is to discover what that destiny is. If you're going to be the kind of leader that can continually manifest new realities, you have to make sure that your intentions are pure, that what you're manifesting is pure for the good of the whole.

The moment when you are informed by Source, there are definite physical and emotional feelings that accompany this. The first is that when it arrives, it arrives whole. It doesn't come in little parts. Number two, the answer has a deep knowing of rightness to it. The test is: When there's any doubt whatsoever, don't act.

Third, you have a sense that time slows down, and your energy is off the charts. The emotions that are attached to it are the rightness and the sense of urgency, the deeper knowing that I cannot, *not* do this. It's my destiny.

Claudia Welss, Citizen Scientist and Board Chair, Institute of Noetic Sciences (California)

"The 'new' science of our interconnected reality has given me reason to believe that we are one of the most important experiments in the universe—if we can develop our innate ability to perceive the expanded reality of our oneness. To me, the essential quality of transcendental leadership is the ability to keep expanding our perception to include more and more of the Whole, and take coherent action within it, so the Whole becomes greater than the sum of our parts.

"At the Institute of Noetic Sciences, our guiding hypothesis is that when we embody this oneness we have access to vast amounts of energy and information contained within this greater Whole. Many of us have learned how to gain access individually (if not reliably!), but transcendental leadership is about helping humanity cultivate the capacity to do so collectively, with no time to waste. What was once considered to be *speculation* about the ultimate unraveling of social and environmental systems is now becoming *our experience*. We are collectively experiencing that if *we* don't change, neither will history—and this time, we could lose it all. What's needed now is a *collective* revelation.

"As a citizen scientist and Chairman of IONS, when it came time for our organization to calibrate our mission statement, I turned to a process that cultivates (what I'm calling) *collective revelation*. The True Purpose Process aims at connecting to the transcendent purpose of an organization, team or person. Over three half days and with two dozen people from across the organization, we utilized our human capacity to perceive the greater Whole *together* and accomplished what we had not been able to accomplish in the previous six months—a collective revelation, with high fidelity, of our IONS mission for the early twenty-first century. Direct experience with such a process helps to realize that while the challenges we face today are urgent, systemic, and far reaching, so are the resources available to help us meet the moment, as long as we operate from the inclusive field of our oneness.

"Captain Edgar Mitchell's epiphany showed him that agape love, or unconditional love, is the organizing principle of the entire cosmos. Science is demonstrating that unconditional love is an organizing principle in our bodies; how far are we from demonstrating that it's also an organizing principle in our world?

I'm not waiting for that scientific proof to discover if unconditional love is an organizing principle in transcendental leadership. I'm already running the experiment, and I encourage you to, too."

Peter Russell, M.S., D.C.S., Author and Faculty Member, Institute of Noetic Sciences (California)

"For me, transcendental leadership is leadership that is grounded in transcendent being. The transcendent is that which transcends all thought, feelings, perceptions, and other mental phenomena. It is the essence of our being, that nameless sense of 'I Am' at the heart of every experience. When I am grounded in my essential being, abiding in the true self, as some would say, my innate wisdom has the opportunity to guide me. This wisdom is universal in that it is available to all. We just have to step back from the thinking mind, which doesn't always have our best interest at heart (much as it would like to think it does). As we drop back towards our true self, our innate wisdom can shine through more freely. My decisions and actions, will be that much freer from the egoic thinking that can often hamper our leadership potential.

"Portals: My primary portal is meditation. Others, such as nature, creativity, and inspired writings, help the journey along.

"Most of my practice these days is what I call micro-meditations. Pausing for a few moments, many times a day. Pausing whatever thought trains I may be following, allowing myself to relax and notice how it feels to pause. Noticing what is here in the present moment. And aware of that transcendent essence, aware that I am that which is aware of all this. Of course, my mind soon kicks in again, but it's not about trying to stay there, but returning many times.

"Traits of a transcendental leader would include calmness, compassion, care, clarity, love, forgiveness, kindness. These are innate potentials of everyone that would no longer be so veiled."

Diane Marie Williams, Founder and President, Source of Synergy Foundation (Netherlands)

"Transcendental leadership begins by tapping into the transcendent in order to surpass our ordinary state of being and lead our lives from this realm of consciousness.

"This form of leadership is about knowing from the depth of one's being that we are all part of a field where we are connected to all that is, all that was, and all that ever will be. Acknowledging, communicating with, trusting, and expressing gratitude for this field and the 'nonlocal coworkers' that permeate it, has informed every aspect of my leadership.

"In 2006, while meditating I heard two words: *source* and *synergy*. Instantaneously, I was intuitively completely clear from a place of deep knowing that a nonprofit organization was about to be born, one that would tap into the Source and create opportunities for synergy from this place.

"The Source of Synergy Foundation was birthed through trusting the clear direction that came from this holographic universal field, and during our fourteen years, we have warmly welcomed the vast intelligences in various realms of existence to partner with us.

"In October 2019, the Source of Synergy Foundation and the Building Bridges Team of the Findhorn Foundation invited twenty-nine colleagues to join a four-day Synergy Circle on Cocreating with the Intelligence of Nature. This gathering tapped into one of the core foundational practices of Findhorn to attune to and collaborate with the vast number of beings that coexist with us on the planet, including our plant and animal friends, spirits of nature, as well as intelligences in other realms of existence, so that we can cocreate a more holistic reality together.

"While at Findhorn, Jonathan Caddy, son of two of its founders, shared with us the story of how his mother, Eileen Caddy, was guided by an inner voice to move to Findhorn, Scotland. This inner voice was so imperative and so strong, that, she and her husband, Peter, and Jonathon and his two brothers, along with the Caddys' good friend Dorothy Maclean, moved to the Moray Coast. Soon after they arrived, they decided they wanted to create a garden. There was one problem, the sandy soil in the region was not conducive to manifesting such a vision.

"During a meditation, Dorothy's inner guidance suggested she begin tapping into the consciousness of nature, including the plants, animals, soil, and elements and partner with the spirits, devas, and angels of the garden, which she saw as embodiments of creative intelligence. As soon as she began to tap in, they started giving her guidance on what was needed for the garden to thrive in spite of the harsh conditions that seemed to make it an impossible feat. Well, they knew the impossible became the possible when they started growing forty-pound cabbages and an abundance of other fruits, vegetables, flowers, herbs, and plants. All of this stunned the scientists, horticulture experts, neighbors and the global community alike because the soil analysis showed that there were not enough nutrients present to produce this outcome.

"Their miraculous garden put Findhorn on the map and it is now a model ecovillage that attracts thousands of visitors each year in part because of the inspiring example of transcendent leadership by its founders.

"The founders of Findhorn were successful in crossing through energetic spheres because of their belief in the ability to communicate with beings in other realms of existence. They understood that this is part of the inheritance of who we really are. We were never meant to be separate from the infinite life forms that exist in other realms, frequencies, and locations in the cosmos and beyond.

"During our Synergy Circle at Findhorn our group of twenty-nine was also successful in tapping into this field through silence, group intentions, and communing directly with nature. Once our extrasensory perceptions and multidimensional abilities became heightened, various intelligences came through to communicate with us, letting us know that they are very much present and wanting to partner with us on bringing back balance, harmony, and hope to our beautiful planet home.

"Transcendental leadership involves sharing these experiences and creating opportunities for others to tap into their multidimensional selves and access higher levels of consciousness so that they can lead the conscious evolutionary movement of global transformation from a place of deep knowing. A knowing based on the knowledge that we can only truly succeed when we embrace and collaborate with the whole of existence in the infinite field of which we are all integral parts."

Roger Tempest, Custodian, Broughton Hall Estate, and Paris Ackrill, Cofounder and Director, Avalon Wellbeing Centre, Broughton Hall Sanctuary (United Kingdom)

"Wanting to be of service is a big anchor for both of us—providing space for nature, healing, community. To us, transcendental leadership means leadership that is of service to the world, guided by Source.

"Creating Avalon was a gradual process of unfolding, coming from a deep listening to what is needed to be done in order to be of service to the world at this time. The concept starts to reveal itself as various things came together. When Truth appears, you know what to do. It feels strongly like being guided by Source.

"Our experience of Source guides our decisions and actions. For our organization, we work on practicing *presence* collectively: for example, by bringing the staff and entire organization present to the moment in order to feel what is real in the now and grasp what needs to be done next. We also work consciously with the energetic architecture of the employees and the property, collaborating and assisting in clearing blocked and stressed energy, and connecting to the information fields that can help us achieve our goals. For instance, at one time, we could feel the external resistance of a negative energy to our tree planting project before it appeared in reality.

"Our primary portals are attunement to nature, regular meditation, and yoga. With this combination, our creativity flows nonstop. We have also been very inspired by Indigenous wisdom, practices, and philosophies. These practices all remind us of our connection to Source, and in particular, of how that connection is channeled through our heart and body.

"A transcendental leader would be a person both connected to Source and the world into which they have chosen to incarnate; passionate about creating greater joy and wholeness in our relative world; and drawing inspiration from the absolute Source.

"For us, Source and service are the pillars of our leadership practice."

Wildrik Timmerman, Cofounder, Mandali Retreat Center (Italy)

"I believe leading is a very gentle process. It's a dance. It is much more about supporting than it is about bluntly telling people what to do. I believe that vision, support, and authentic interest are the main parts of it. Once you give people a sense of direction that speaks to them, that they can see and feel, there is nothing more to do than to support them in playing their individual role in the process of working towards that vision.

"To put it in simple words: getting out of the way. The less I'm identified with my egoic patterns, the more I'm able to 'sense and feel' what needs support.

"Portals: Practicing *presence* is my main portal to tune in. I walk around with my 'insight timer' app all day, reminding me every fifteen minutes to stop and be present.

"Traits: presence and knowing: It's hard to talk about without sounding as if I think I know anything about it. Whereas the truth is that I am just learning. Every day. I feel that when I am in deep presence, knowing happens. It's not so much that I have to obtain information, the information is just there. It's about being open to it, 'knowing' it. When it happens, it's beautiful. But also, many times, it does not happen. At least not when I want it. And that's just the point. Not wanting. Wanting is of the mind. Knowing is of the heart. Other key traits, as I said, are support, getting out of the way, positivity, and perseverance.

"Rituals: Invitation is one of them. Inviting each staff member, at every possible occasion, to talk; we are always available to talk about work situations and private situations. Taking the time for just for a cup of coffee or a glass of wine. In this way, whenever they have a question, issue, or challenge, we are available. This allows us to be supportive of their needs.

"Wouter, my cofounder at Mandali and long-time friend, and I always hold a positive perspective; we're never defeated and always looking at a bright and interesting future. Always growing. Like life."

Anne-Marie Voorhoeve, Founder and Director, Hague Center for Global Governance (Netherlands)

"The notion of transcendental leadership is like a symphony orchestra. The conductor plays an essential role in leading and *allowing* the musicians to play together by *orchestrating* the rhythm and structure—coordinating when to, for example, play soft or loud in coherence with archetypal emotion to inspire and stir the listening audience.

"In addition to the conductor, the musician plays a key role. They need to align with the maestro's interpretation and be willing to follow. There are external agreements of course, the rules of the game so to say, but the individual, their commitment, and internal agreements make the difference.

"To further the analogy, it all starts with attunement. Each musician must attune their instruments to the collectively decided tone that is at the core of the score, the tone ladder. Without that, no matter what the conductor does, it will not sound as *one*, collectively energized, and transcendence-making musical experience.

"There is an international agreement on the standard hertz frequency that creates the harmony provided by tuning forks. In the moments just before the concert starts, the lead violinist and oboe listen to that and tune their instruments accordingly. The more accurately the better. This important skill and capacity requires a practice in deep, present, listening. And then, just before the maestro steps up on the podium facing the orchestra, there is a moment of attention, and in the silence, these leaders play the one note repeatedly. The intention and attention of each individual musician must be to listen carefully to that one note and tune their instruments to that tonal key with accuracy."

Esperide Ananas Ametista, Spokesperson, Temples of Humankind (Italy)

"Transcendental leaders are leaders of all times and all kinds are people who can tell a beautiful story. Or that can have someone tell a beautiful story for them, while they remain ever mysterious and perceived as the source of inspiration beyond the veil. Being a leader is not a role, it is a dynamic relationship. Without a compelling narrative, you can have the most brilliant ideas, or even the ability to see the future, but nobody will listen, nobody will follow. So, transcendent leadership requires a compelling, transcendental story, one so profound, exciting and interesting to engage in a relationship with the hearts and minds of others, so that they feel the connection with their spirit more strongly.

"With the world changing ever faster, I believe that everyone who wants to be a leader, inspire others, and teach—at all levels— needs to have the humility of learning constantly. A leader with a spiritual purpose is one that knows how to listen to the pure wisdom of children, and to the often-disruptive narrative of adolescents—through their words, their music, and the TV series they love. If we think of every human as a mix of energies and alchemical ingredients, the youth contain more future than adults. And the elderly contain more history, so a good leader treasures their voices, too.

"We need leaders to tell a story that can inspire a complete redesign. In our times, transcendence marries matter to bring Spirit into every aspect of our lives. If you can imagine it, you can make it. Manifestation always follows intention; matter always obeys consciousness. Some of the indispensable ingredients are acting locally, returning to a way of living in harmony with nature and the Earth, growing and feeding on local products rich in life and the substances that we need to keep our body healthy, and taking back sovereignty of our health by taking care of the body as the seat of our soul. We also need to unite the masculine and feminine within us to be complete individuals, who are truly capable of loving— beyond all definitions of gender—and create new formulas for relationships and family. We need to surround ourselves with art and music, not only as users but experiencing the pleasure and the courage to all be creators. We need to give life to intentional and regenerative communities everywhere, even in cities. We need to support and create alternative information networks and create complementary local currency systems. We need to support small businesses most affected by the economic crisis that lockdowns are creating [*editor's note:* this interview took place in early 2021] and create a virtuous economy respectful of human beings and the world. Finally, we need to have the courage to unite and make our voice heard, in all the streets of the world, both physical and virtual.

"If we all manage to take a spiritual leap, after the tempest, we will discover a sky bright with the colors of a new dawn. Bringing this sky to life, alive with as many details as possible, is what a transcendental leader can now do with their storytelling.

"Zen Master and poet Thich Nhat Hanh said: "The next Buddha will be a community." I believe that only in community we can find a new optimistic story for the future."

Judi Weisbart, President and Founder, Busy Woman Consulting (California)

"*Transcendental leadership* refers to those who believe that their leadership and role in the world is a partnership with a higher source. If we listen to the inner voice in our hearts, we will choose the correct road to travel and the correct way to communicate on this journey we call life.

"What I call the inner voice we hear when we are willing to listen to the deep wisdom that we can all connect with if we chose is the ancient wisdom that permeates the world. When we really listen with our ears, hearts, and minds to information embedded in the religious traditions, the history of the peoples, and the voices of the ancestors, we learn to 'see' in a different way.

"We are all connected and the universal power of wisdom is not to be taken lightly. It is the one thing that we could depend on if we chose to experience its power and grandeur.

"My portals are nature, creativity, relationship, and service.

"Nature: To me, the gift of water allows my body to move and my mind to become quiet. I swim most days and as I do I say prayers for the world. I have done this practice for over thirty years and it is my portal to the quiet wisdom I seek. With each lap in the pool or strokes in the ocean, I pray. They are prayers from many wisdom traditions. I do them in the same order each day beginning with Hindu, then I go on to Jewish, Christian, Buddhist, Moslem, and Native American, and then to positive affirmations for health, abundance for all my loved ones, the world at peace, and so on. This allows me to see in my mind's eye a vast and beautiful tapestry of humanity, animals, and the planet. I pray for it all and for all that will be.

"Creativity: My blessing in life is that I am a creative. My passion is to get lost or enter the space of the creator and make art.

"Relationship: This is a portal that can teach us more than we can ever imagine if we stay open and hear what is really being said. I have an almost fifty-year marriage, I am the mother to three stepchildren and one biological son, the grandma to two amazing people and all of them are sources of wisdom. I have been blessed with amazing friends, and the most exceptional people from my work in nonprofits, medicine, and faith communities, to those who are business gurus and philanthropists. I am always in awe of the people I work and play with, who support me mind, body and heart. Relationship is the true meaning of universal wisdom, being surrounded by a multitude of voices that want to be a part of your world and want you to be a part of theirs. They give me meaning, love, wisdom, support, and a deep feeling of gratitude.

"Service: How could I live on this beautiful radiant globe if not in constant service to it and all who live with me. *Service is my oxygen.* It is the reason I get up each day and the reason I feel blessed each night. Service is the physical manifestation of faith and joy. It is the purpose that powers my life because when I am of service, I feel happy. Service is how we can pay the rent for the gift of life."

"I think there are a couple of traits necessary to be a transcendental leader. The first is to love, respect, and show compassion for human beings. Without these feelings, it will be impossible to lead as no one will follow in any consistent, meaningful way. The other trait one needs to lead is by listening to those who are connected to your team, group, business, or community.

"The only good leadership is the manifestation of a group consciousness. This happens when a community of some kind rallies around you and wants to connect and be bigger and better together. When a leader feels that their work is to inspire, connect and be of service to a greater whole they make real the idea of transcendental leadership."

Agapi Stassinopoulos, Speaker, Author, and Trainer, Thrive Global (New York and California)

"Leadership starts inside of us, and we need to gain mastery over the lower levels of our consciousnesses so we can tap into Spirit. When we are connected with our higher wisdom, with our higher purpose, we can become amazing, powerful, and impactful leaders for others. This is because we are operating from the consciousness of oneness. From this mindset, we inherently know that what is most important is *serving the highest good of all*—and therefore, we can make decisions that impact the good of all; and to me, that is what a true leader is."

"Portals: I think the practice of contemplation and meditation, of silently listening to one's inner guidance, is the foundation of a centered and grounded human being. Taking time every day to attune to the deep silence and stillness within, where we can be open to receiving moment-to-moment guidance, helps us operate on a higher frequency and mindset. From this place of calmness and clarity we can be extremely effective in providing thoughtful solutions—and joy—to ourselves and others. A daily practice of some sort that reconnects us to our center is essential and I believe must be brought to the forefront of an educational system.

"I also believe that sincere and present listening allows others to be who they are by giving them the respect of where they are right now in their lives before we jump in to impose our own thoughts and feelings. In this way, we offer a safe space for others to express their concerns, their opinions, and their views of being. It fundamentally comes to letting others be where they are and loving ourselves where we are and then bringing the spirit of wisdom, kindness, reverence, and humility to ourselves and to others."

"Traits: There are six traits that I think a leader must possess:

- Knowing what it is to serve human beings in the consciousness of oneness.
- Being spirit driven rather than ego driven.
- Humility of accepting the things he or she doesn't know.
- Encouraging others in becoming the best version of themselves.
- Shedding light on those who are discriminated against and have no voice.

"A true leader is a person who has a great purpose to serve the good of all.

"Ritual: I love to start every meeting, no matter how small or big and whether it is in person or on zoom, with a moment of centering. I encourage others to come into a moment of conscious breathing, disconnecting from the thing they did last, to come fully present to serve this gathering and this meeting with their whole selves. This way, every interaction and every meeting becomes an impactful connection. We are bringing our whole selves to our next actions, solutions, or whatever the agenda is about.

Judith Skutch Whitson, Founder and Chairwoman of the Board, Foundation for Inner Peace (California)

"*A Course in Miracles* [published by the Foundation for Inner Peace] is a book in three sections. It contains a text, a workbook

174

for students, and a teacher's manual, which doesn't mean that a teacher outside of your realm is going to teach you but rather that *you* will be connecting with your inner teacher which is your highest self—the Holy Spirit, or whatever you want to call it. The lessons to practice every day are opportunities to see that forgiveness is the key to happiness. When I learned that, from that point on I realized that the leadership in my life was always there and had nothing to do with me looking outside myself. It was inside me, in my higher self, my inner teacher."

"Portals: What I have noticed works for people would be willingness. Asking for guidance and being willing to receive it is a very important thing. I love this line from the *Course*. "Show the slightest willingness and a thousand angels rush in to help." It intimates that we are not just bodily forms going through our daily lives trying to survive as best we can, but there are other supporting forces. And that when we ask for the help of other forces "a thousand angels rush in to help." When you are willing to relinquish the control of being right and realize you'd much rather be happy, another way is always found.

"Nature: I think nature's something we all agree on. I can't imagine anyone who doesn't like what's growing on our planet or being out on a sunny day looking at the ocean. I mean, you can get mesmerized looking at the ocean. This is one of the most wonderful meditations you can do. You just set your mind in a flow with it and, before long, something creeps over you and you feel you're a part of it. You recognize your oneness with all that is. You may be a drop in the ocean, but you're also the whole ocean.

"I recommend *all* the practices and methods that lead to the remembrance of our oneness.

"Traits: In its manual for teachers, *A Course in Miracles* lists ten attributes of a teacher of God, which, it says, we all are. The attributes have to do with patience and kindness, receptivity, awareness of oneness, gentleness. There's a whole bunch of them. Peaceful. A person who listens. Love.

"I was lucky enough to meet Mother Teresa because she was a very good friend of the two course scribes. She turned her attention to me to find out who I was and asked what my life was like. I told her that I had recently been through a very difficult time where I felt like I was spiraling down although I had everything. There was no reason for me to feel so empty and so unhappy. And she said, 'Oh darling, there was.'

"I said, 'Really?'

"She said, 'You were suffering from a disease. It's called *spiritual deprivation* and it's endemic in this society.'

"I said, 'Spiritual deprivation? That sounds very right. If it's endemic, is there a cure?'

"She looked at me and said, 'Yes, it's called love—and it's contagious.'

"As simple as that. Mother Teresa's message was to love each other. 'If you can't do it with the poorest of the poor of the world, as I do, do it with your family, do it with your mate, do it with your children. If you can't do that, do it with ideas and try to bring yourself into a state of lovingness.'"

Peter Matthies, Founder and CEO, Conscious Business Institute (California)

"For me, transcendental leadership is when you lead from a place of universal wisdom as compared to traditional leadership, which commonly operates from a place of limitation and control. Even in the best form of traditional leadership, the idea to 'get people to do something' is essentially manipulation. The desire is to reach a certain, mind-made outcome usually to the benefit of one or a relatively small group of people: the leader, the board of an organization, its shareholders, and so forth.

"Transcendental leaders operate from a higher level of consciousness, an 'us'-centric, global-centric or universe-centric perspective. With this different level of consciousness, they operate in service to a higher wisdom, including universal principles, intuition, and an understanding of interconnectedness.

"My portals include frequent time in nature, meditation (I do formal meditation for twenty minutes daily and take other opportunities to meditate with audios), and movement practices that include yoga, dance, and aikido.

"My practices—done consistently—help me in several ways: They provide the space and practice to *be*, to empty the mind and establish space for a higher connection. I engage in these practices with an intention to connect, to receive information, and to access a higher wisdom.

"When I am consulting and leading, I personally check in by accessing a higher wisdom before meetings, coaching sessions, and client engagements. I always receive additional wisdom or information during these check-ins, sometimes to the point that I feel uncomfortable sharing the information with the client. Yet, every time I have done so, it has hit the mark with them.

"I believe that the transcendental leader exhibits the following traits. No ego (ideally). Clear discernment, but without judgment. Emotional balance, resilience, and intelligence. Oneness mindset. Acceptance of what-is, combined with a commitment to serve humanity.

"People tell me that I create space where people can expand, with little judgment, safety, kindness, and compassion, together with the ability to provide insight.

"Ritual: I request that everyone on the team, in the group, or participating in a training/retreat check in together before we start. This helps to create the space for context conversations (how are we/how do we work together) instead of only content conversations.

"My conviction is that if we listened to transcendental knowledge more, as leaders and organizations, we would save an enormous amount of time and hardship."

John Renesch, Author and Founder, Conscious Leadership Guild (California)

"My label for transcendental leadership is *conscious leadership.* There are many labels created by many authors and consultants over the years. My notion of what this means is a combination of self-actualized awareness *plus* responsible action based on that awareness. Consciousness defies definition; it is ineffable. But the human mind likes to define things, so it continually tries to 'eff' the ineffable. In my view, a notion is a better description than a definition when it comes to this dimension of reality.

"My portals include meditation, to be sure! I also check in with my ineffable source of guidance from time to time. I also have a twelve-step process that gives me grounding in my practice. I volunteer a lot in the spirit of service. I find nature, Indigenous wisdom, inspirational writings, intimate relationships, and yoga to be quite liberating and inspiring."

Peter Merry, Ph.D., Cofounding Chief Innovation Officer, Ubiquity University, Speaker, and Author (Netherlands)

"Transcendental leadership is leadership that transcends, yet includes, the material and relational realms. That engages explicitly and consciously with the subtle energetic fields, in connection with the material and relational. I bridge my work with these fields by using energetic balancing processes and allowing myself to be guided by intuition in decision-making and planning.

"Portals: Embodiment practices and quieting my analytic mind reconnects me to my body and opens up my intuitive knowing. Plus, meditation, knowing, and Indigenous wisdom. Service, inspired writings, and nature."

"Traits: Presence, being with what is, and sensing into what *wants* to happen next."

Juliet Rohde Brown, Ph.D., Doctoral Chair of Integrative Therapy and Healing Practices, Pacifica Graduate Institute (California)

"The strong transcendental leaders I have observed have the capacity to stand steady in the face of adversity, to meet each person as a unique and worthy being, and to listen authentically, pause for reflection, and respond in nonharmful ways. Sometimes difficult things need to be communicated, but even if those communications are painful to hear, they are not harmful. The qualities of embodying a middle way of understanding situations and engaging in skillful communication and heart-centeredness and doing so authentically and assertively can make profound differences in the lives of those who are fortunate enough to know and work with such a leader.

"I bridge my organizational and relationship decisions with my spiritual awareness by trying to be consistent with how I show up in life regardless of the context. Thus, how I might respond to, say, a conflictual situation in my organizational setting is congruent with how I respond in my marriage or other interpersonal relationships. Sometimes I slow down and I breathe into my heart center and feel into an energetic intention of each of our hearts connecting at the subtle level. When I do this, there is a visceral shift and grounding in my body while at the same time opening to a kind of expansiveness. I engage in meditative practices that nurture an impartial beneficence for all beings. In this way, I can pick myself up with compassion when I make mistakes and I build my capacity to stay in a place of compassion with those who may even commit egregious acts, while not condoning those acts. I look to the context, not just the content.

"I see this as a continual learning as I stumble along the path of life in my humanness. Thus, I value the concept of beginner's mind and practices that cultivate more spaciousness of mind and heart. We all have shadow aspects as well, so it is how we meet them that makes all the difference in our interpersonal interactions whether these relationships be personal or professional."

"Ritual: I begin each class or meeting with a meditation and sometimes a poem. I encourage those in the room or video conferencing call to pause into their body and center in the heart area and to fully arrive before moving into any material at hand. I try to bring all voices to the table. I advocate for those who have been marginalized. I imagine spiritual guides in a circle of care around us.

"Also, we have a labyrinth on our campus at Pacifica Graduate Institute. It was created to represent the arms and legs of a Chumash Goddess reaching out to both the mountains and the sea toward the Santa Cruz islands. There are several places outdoors on our campus that we gather and a cherished individual who is part of our program is a Chumash elder who often leads us in Native American ceremonies for special occasions, such as orientation, solstice and equinox days, and the completion of coursework.

"We encourage our students to lead us in ritual as well. For instance, one of our students acknowledged that several students in her cohort had lost loved ones and she asked if she could create a grieving ritual for a weekend of both quiet time in individual solitude and group ceremony. She created a space under one of the mulberry trees, brought slips of mulberry paper from an elder in South Korea, and people wrote their grief onto these slips and hung them on the tree. There was an opening ceremony that she and our Chumash elder led and at the closing ceremony, she had everyone remove their slips of paper from the tree. Circling around with a singing bowl full of water, each person dropped their slip of paper into the water. She led a meditation, invited people to share, and closed with a beautiful blessing. She was to take the paper and make a sculpture out of the shared grieving as a remembrance of the ritual."

Patty DeDominic, CEO and Founder, DeDominic and Associates (California)

"To me, transcendental leadership means not assuming anything ahead of encounters and being open to new ideas, strategies, and tactics.

"Portals: Sometimes I pray and work to learn more when I am not immediately clear on how or what to do.

"Traits: integrity, empathy, willingness to listen and to learn every day. Capacity to suspend. I have learned that it sometimes best to do nothing and allow circumstances and people to unfold. Just because I *can* do something absolutely does not mean that I should do it or will do it. I carefully weigh options and potential unintended consequences when I am problem solving or helping business leaders that I coach. I believe in empowering others. We can do that by listening to them and helping them see a broader picture, or if they are stuck, we can help them get unstuck by illuminating other facts and feelings. We can help draw the wisdom out of people, and for ourselves by listening, working to understand others and our environment.

"Intuition and experience also help me know when to act and when to listen. As a CEO, I have had to listen to many people from all walks of my business and personal life. At times I have been confident, and at times, willing to be vulnerable and ask for help. I carefully choose those whom I associate with for their integrity, sense of humor, industriousness, and especially those who are on a worthy mission."

Catherine Butler, Founder, At the Chapel Retreat Centre (United Kingdom)

"I've always been challenged by the awareness that most of the damage in our world is being done by the way we do business from a model of control, causing much stress and leading us to feel powerless. So, my thinking around this has always been, 'What can I do?' and more and more the growing feeling is that 'I can do better business' and be part of the growing global movement of business as a force for good.

"A friend said to me: 'A good business is not so much about ownership; it is more about relationship.' I came to realize that ownership is a manmade concept created in the matrix. It doesn't exist in nature. In nature, nothing owns anything—it's all about relationship.

"And so, here we are. Now. In a time where a coronavirus has brought about an unprecedented global shutdown resulting in the closure of many businesses. Even so, the limits on us are not where we think they are. There is some untapped potential within us that, if realized, empowers us to not just survive through difficult times but to thrive.

"We must come to realize how we are connected through nature, and that we are part of that natural environment in which something develops. Intelligent connection. Nature is so intelligent and connected and we are so deeply connected to this world. There's a harmony in this world based on energy. The energy of the field. All information is in the field and we are the field. We are here to create. To create something beautiful.

"The information is coming in from the outside. Our intuition is downloaded from another realm and all exploration begins with intuition. These discoveries expand our understanding of who we really are and lead us to a deeper understanding of ourselves.

"The answers lie within."

We would certainly characterize a number of spiritual leaders, like His Holiness the Dalai Lama, and some individuals working hard in social activism as transcendental leaders. I'd like to share the stories of many others, but unfortunately, in researching these leaders I too often found that there was almost nothing said anywhere about their interests in accessing universal wisdom or cultivating presence.

I personally would love to learn more about the portals and presences of people like:

Jacinda Ardern, Prime Minister, New Zealand

Stacey Abrams, Founder, Fair Fight

Nury Turkel, Commissioner, U.S. Commission on International Religious Freedom

MacKenzie Scott, Philanthropist

Malala Yousafzai, Cofounder, Malala Fund

I was disappointed to learn (or I should say, *not* learn) that the stories in the media about these aforementioned individuals, don't say anything about a component to their lives that alludes to an interest in a higher consciousness or spiritual awareness. I can only assume that some of them have a portal they utilize to access the states of transcendence that provide a conduit to being informed by Source. It's too bad that they, or their publicists, or the journalists covering them feel that it's not an aspect of them to share with the world.

Sure, there are a few high-profile leaders who proselytize mindfulness in their companies. We are familiar with those people, so I don't need to list them here.

In addition, it's been a bit dicey navigating which leaders in big-business to interview and highlight, because so many seem to have the kind of egos which aren't aligned with this topic. As you recall, humility is one of the primary traits. Transcendental leaders do not posture or brag. They have nothing-to-prove.

Lastly, I do want to highlight an individual who I believe is a transcendental leader and a wonderful soul model, as Jude

Currivan would say, that I did not get a chance to interview. This leader is Jean Houston, Ph.D.

Let's start with a wonderful story that Jean likes to tell, about her encounter in Central Park in 1951 with the renowned French Jesuit, paleontologist, theologian and philosopher Pierre Teilhard de Chardin. When she was fourteen years old, purely by chance, she befriended the elderly man. In the passage below, she describes an exchange with "Mr. Tayer," as she calls him, in which he shared his spiritual interpretation of evolution.

> *"We need to have more specialists in spirit who will lead people into self-discovery," he told me.*
>
> *"What do you mean, Mr. Tayer?"*
>
> *He said—and this is exactly what he said, as I was taking notes because I knew I was in the presence of greatness. "We are being called into metamorphosis, into a far higher order, and yet we often act only from a tiny portion of ourselves. It is necessary that we increase that portion. But do not think for one minute, Jean, that we are alone in making that possible. We are part of a cosmic evolutionary movement that inspires us to unite with God. This is the lightning flash for all our potentialities. This is the great originating cause of all our shifts and changes."*[1]

Her synchronistic meeting with de Chardin struck the chord of transcendence that propelled her toward her life purpose. She is long regarded as one of the principal founders of the Human Potential Movement and is noted for her ability to combine a deep knowledge of history, culture, new science, spirituality, and human development into her teaching. Her lifetime passion has been to encourage the inherent possibilities, visions, and capacities that lie within each person and/or group and translate them into positive action.

Dr. Houston demonstrates transcendental leadership through her commitment to leading a movement that inspires every individual to embrace their full potential and to create a life of purpose. Her self-knowledge is a fundamental building block of her effective leadership and *way of being*. She is a self-aware and selfless leader whose organization cultivates and teaches introspective inquiry and contemplative practices to self-actualize ourselves. In this way, the student/follower becomes aligned with their own calling to serve the welfare of humanity and the world.

In a *Huffington Post* article in 2010 on the "Future of God," Dr. Houston said:

We are now at that crossroads between biology and cosmology. We are called to explore the mystery itself as an interface between engagement with external realities and embracing the inner journey. This brings us to a place of contemplative practice, and the vital synergy between inner and outer realities necessary to transform self, institutions, paths of possibility, as well as visionary endeavors. And in so doing, unleash the human spirit of those who compose the institution or endeavor and of those who are served by this. It is an activity of extraordinary balance, a tension in repose. It is about a zone in which paradox occurs. It is a space where the sacred emerges and the local self disappears. It is a space of exquisite silence and of extraordinary service. It is a space wherein there is a fusing and blending of silence and service. In such a state one has access to the creative, world making place where one's unique entelechy (the essential self) meets the entelechy of a potential new time, one that gives the details of an evolution in person and society."[2]

The transcendental leader may prefer not to lead an organization that espouses greed and/or reductionist obscurantism, but that is why a new narrative of leadership is necessary. It may be too late for many of the leaders of today to become self-actualized, but it is not too late for new leaders and the development of new leadership training emerging today.

The potential for widespread spiritual awakening—the inner science of being—is occurring all over the world today. Due to our rapidly evolving communications technology, information is continually being shared faster than ever before and connecting more people in remote locations of the planet. Can we at last be reaching the critical mass of awakening people required for the transformational shift we need? I am hopeful.

The heroic soul does not sell its justice and its nobleness, it does not ask to dine nicely, and to sleep warm. The essence of greatness is the perception that virtue is enough.[3]
—*Ralph Waldo Emerson*

REFLECTION EXERCISE

Having read the words and accounts of my survey respondents and interview subjects:

- Which of the voices above did you find most compelling and resonant?
- What area of service to the world are you personally interested in contributing to?
- Combining the portals and traits you possess with the contributions you want to make, is a certain path illuminated for you?
- Which of these individuals could be a soul model for you? Why?

EPILOGUE
WHERE CAN WE GO FROM
HERE?

The place where courage and commitment meet with
Source is the moment and intersection that you engage
with your destiny.
—Susan Taylor, cofounder and CEO,
Generon International

What are the implications for the contribution and benefits of transcendental leadership to the governance of organizations in the education, business, and nonprofit sectors of our society? Where can we go from here? Wherever we go, we must go together and be guided by higher thought.

The current phase of Earth history is being defined by the presence of humanity. We've created the mess we're in. To paraphrase Roger Walsch, Ph.D.:

Our global problems are actually global symptoms:
symptoms of our individual and collective psychological
dysfunctions. The state of the world reflects the state of our
minds. We are in a race between consciousness and
catastrophe.[1]

Since 2020, we've been in a surging and resurging global pandemic, exacerbated periodically by all manner of institutional dysfunction and failures. This state of affairs is an example of how hard it is to create consensus and collaboration even in the face of a common threat. Of course, organizations are not democracies, even those that operate within democratic nations. For the most part, they are authoritarian, managed as top-down hierarchies. With power resting in the hands of an elite few individuals, the tone of the leaders defines the culture of the company. Many people at different levels of corporations and organizations feel like they are increasingly unable to achieve their visions, missions, and purposes. Corporations seem to ignore the increasingly precarious wellbeing of our planet because they continue to embrace the old paradigm of increased growth and expansion at all costs. And government leaders seem willing to do the same. The private sector interests are often enmeshed with the public sector interests in the United States and other developed western nations, and people feel enormous stress in the face of these challenges.

Clearly, we are living in a time of crisis that demands a new consciousness and narrative about leadership. In an era when the paradigm of leadership could be shifting, it is the time to embrace the leading-edge wisdom of emergence and coherence. It is time to rely less on the transactional, bureaucratic, hierarchical leader and empower the interconnected, collectively oriented transcendental leader who is tuned in and turned on by their intuitive knowledge of the frequency of their pioneering emergence with Source, or if you prefer, with universal wisdom.

Let us endorse the paradigm—and narrative—of consciously aware and wisdom-based leadership exemplified by inspired thinking, being, and doing.

It is my contention that as long as the prevailing systems and values of business and governance rule our organizations—the old *ways of doing,* such as control, standardization, growth, growth, growth and "faster is better" —we will continue not only to recreate systems imbued with disconnection and disharmony, but also continue to turn a blind eye to the devastation of our planet, allowing its resources to be depleted for the benefit of a few and to the detriment of our children and the entire global population—every living creature. Whereas if we allow transcendental principles to guide us, we stand a chance of developing new, more beneficial systems and timely solutions.

People and those who lead them tend to limit themselves by defining themselves and being informed by their worldviews, their pasts, and what they believe they can or cannot do. From the heart and soul of the individual, either disharmony and disconnection or harmony and connection emanate throughout the organization, families, societies, communities, and into the larger cosmology. Systems have to evolve to end the chaos and meet the challenges of our era. So, we must begin to envision what we might *become* and not what we have been.

It's difficult to envision and learn new ways of doing, being, and interacting when most of our learning and decision making has been reactive. This is especially true when people know that they have to respond to circumstances they didn't have any input in creating in the first place. Reactive management and decision-making are usually governed by old, habitual ways of thinking, and seeing situations through familiar, comfortable lenses. Reactive leaders usually discount new options and interpretations that differ from those with which they are familiar. Their default *modus operandi* is to defend their interests and "be right." This is when a trait we discussed in Chapter 3 becomes invaluable: the capacity to suspend.

A new mode of thinking is possible. New ways of learning integrate thinking, *being*, and doing. New ways of thinking, *being*, and learning can evolve from how we relate, and from the capacities that are developed from those interactions. In reactive leadership, our *doing* is informed by habits of action. In transcendental leadership, our deeper levels of wisdom and insight contribute to our conscious awareness and desire to serve the whole—both as it is and as it might evolve to be—and therefore our actions can increasingly create alternative modes of effectiveness. We are thinking, *being*, and intuiting out of the box, so to speak. Until our wisdom and awareness reaches beyond superficial events and circumstances, our thinking, being, and actions will remain reactive.

The beauty is that we get to choose the model of leadership that suits us best. As B. Alan Wallace, Ph.D., the founder and president of the Santa Barbara Institute for Consciousness Studies, says:

The skill of directing and sustaining attention is more than a marvelous ability; it is the cornerstone of understanding and choosing the reality we wish to experience.[2]

Transcendental leaders envision new worldviews and modes of thought. They operate from a deep connection to inherent universal wisdom and the Implicate Order and with awareness of the divine nature of themselves and others, including all life forms, and reality. We're talking about their way of *being*.

To me, the bottom line to is for leaders to help everyone else be in resonant alignment with Source and universal wisdom, which includes them helping other people cultivate presence and awareness too, and helping people find avenues and paths to be in service to the whole.

I ask again: Where do we go from here? If we can, we ought to attend to the next generation more astutely. Aware parents tend to raise aware children. (This works in reverse too.) Aware people can, in fact, raise the frequencies of their families, friends, communities, and organizations. If we want to learn to become more aware, then we need to learn how. This kind of learning can be found in numerous ways. If this idea appeals to you, go back and review the portals in Chapter 4. Evaluate which of those gateways resonate with you and then practice them until they become second nature.

There are currently many leadership courses, college degrees, and certificate programs popping up all over the world in credentialed and noncredentialled formats. Some of their curricula skirt the issue of the portals, perhaps perceiving them as too far outside conventions. However, there are many couched in the vernaculars of mindful leadership, conscious leadership, and transformational leadership. These orientations are slowly leading us in the right direction.

All the practices inherent to transcendental leadership could be developed within formal educational programs as much as through informal learning opportunities, such as webinars, social network streaming, online summits, retreats, and workshops. Transcendence could be put into place through leadership and management courses at colleges and universities, as well as delivered within corporate, nonprofit, community, and governance training programs.

It should be noted that advanced leadership training within this model must be facilitated by transcendental leaders who have attained a holistic and subtle stage of self-actualization and development themselves. Although, as I mentioned at the beginning of the book, we can gain self-realization suddenly, it is unlikely. It customarily takes years of consistent contemplative practice, employing one or more of the portals discussed in Chapter 4, such as meditation, movement, exposure to nature, and so on. The transcendental leadership teacher will innately energetically infuse program participants with their own capacity for extraordinary functioning and performance. At the heart of their being, they have the capacity to access tacit knowing—the underlying intelligence within the universe. This ability can be used for the kind of guidance, breakthrough thinking, strategic planning, and innovation (including envisioning and preparing for future scenarios) that our organizations, institutions, and society need.

I can't encourage you enough to discover and dig into your favorite practices for aligning your frequency with Source, the all-encompassing source of love and compassion and universal wisdom. Nurture and share your leadership traits. Increase your awareness, embrace the present moment, and serve the world.

And if you want some help, contact me. I'm committed to serving you!

Shawne Mitchell
shawne@soulstyle.com

ACKNOWLEDGMENTS

At the top of the list, I'm enormously grateful for the guiding soul and longtime friendship of my editor, Stephanie Gunning. Thank you for your patience and expertise. You are the best!

As most mothers know, our children are such unanticipated, yet fortuitous and astonishing teachers for us parents. It certainly has been true for me. My sons, Travis and Austin Cook, are deeply treasured and beloved. Their love and support are foundational to me. I'm also grateful to the entire "cast of characters" of my brothers and their families. In particular, brother Mitch (King, Jr.), has been a hero to me. He knows . . .

Grazie mille to my dear friends Wildrik Timmerman and Wouter Tavecchio, the cofounders of the Mandali Retreat Center in Italy. In particular, Wildrik, I cherish you. *Namaste* for your *always loving* kindness, friendship, and support. My time at Mandali is a treasured chapter of my life.

After escaping the pandemic in Italy in 2020 and finding my way back to the States, and after quarantining in Tucson with brother Mitch, my longtime friend, soul sister, and intrepid college travel companion, Dianne Iverson, gave me her house (nestled amid the evergreen forests, archipelago islands, snow-capped Olympic Mountains and the salty seaport villages west of Seattle on the Olympic Peninsula) to peacefully sequester and write this book. It was a quiet covid winter spent navigating writing, meditating, and some safe playtime with our families and close friends. Thanks, Di!

Thank you, Patty DeDominic, for your kind generosity in providing retreat at your lovely ranch in Santa Ynez, California as the final elements of this book were being crafted.

It is such a special honor to have Joseph Jaworski and Susan Taylor write the foreword to this book. There are no words that can adequately describe my gratitude to you both. Joseph and Susan are passionate advocates for leadership aligned with and guided by Source. Thank you so much!

Decades of study chronicle the long journey of writing this book. Along the way, I have met many people that have influenced me in different ways. I must share that when I originally wrote my master's thesis there was a chapter highlighting individuals who embodied the traits and attributes of transcendental leadership. My professors and advisors requested that I should only highlight a small handful, and that they should be social activists that had lived in the modern era, extraordinary leaders like Mohandas K. Gandhi, the Dalai Lama, Nelson Mandela, and Rev. Dr. Martin Luther King, Jr. For this book, I wanted to include individuals who are "in the trenches," so to speak, people with their feet-on-the-ground *today*. Basically, people like you and I, working and caring about the wellbeing of our communities and planet, doing our best to lead lives with the sincere focus and intention of leading informed by and aligned with universal wisdom and the loving guidance of Source.

Let me take a moment here to express my heartfelt gratitude and to present the remarkable people who shared their inestimable thoughts and experiences of embodying the traits and qualities of transcendental leaders. Much of what is written in this book has been generously offered by these wise and kind individuals: Agapi Stassinopoulos, Catherine Butler, Claudia Welss, Diane Marie Williams, Esperide Ananas Ametista, Eve Konstantine, Heather Shea, Jim Garrison, Joseph Jaworski, John Renesch, Jude Currivan, Judi Weisbart, Judith Skutch Whitson, Juliet Rhode-Brown, Marie-Anne Voorhoeve, Paris Ackrill, Patty DeDominic, Peter Matthies, Peter Merry, Peter Russell, Roger Temple, Roger Walsh, Stephen Rechtschaffen, Susan Taylor, and Wildrik Timmerman.

I've researched and shared quotes and comments of others as well. However, I want to especially thank the aforementioned people for their kind willingness to review my interview questions and share their thoughts and experiences. There are bios and contact information to be found within for those whose remarks are cited at length.

I extend special thanks to Peter Russell who was kind enough to brainstorm with me in fine-tuning the primary portals for accessing states of transcendence. Also, deep thanks to my longtime dear friend Christian de Quincey for his insightful thoughts and ideas and Juliet Rohde-Brown for her discerning suggestions, as well.

Special heart-love gratitude to Satsuki Nona Mitchell, my extraordinary and amazing niece, for the spectacular photograph she took in Careyes, Mexico, which beautifully graces the cover of the book; and Gus Yoo, graphic designer extraordinaire who designed the cover! Thank you.

This book has been years in the making. The first *download* and notion of the idea of Transcendental Leadership came to me in 2013, when it was time to submit a proposal for my Master's thesis in Consciousness Studies. I received a tremendous amount of guidance and direction from several of my professors: Professor Debashish Banerji, Ph.D., former university president at UPRS, and currently Haidas Chaudhuri Professor of Indian Philosophies and Cultures at the California Institute of Integral Studies, where he is also the chair of the East-West Psychology department; Christian de Quincey, Ph.D., former Dean of the Consciousness Studies program at UPRS and popular author; Richard G. Geldard, Ph.D., author and philosophy professor; and B. Alan Wallace, Ph.D., Professor of Buddhist studies and founder of the Santa Barbara Institute for Consciousness Studies. Lastly, in memorandum, CEO of the University of Philosophical Research, Los Angeles, Dr. Obadiah Harris.

We can't always know when the timing is right for something to *want to* emerge and serve our world. Even when I was studying, researching, and writing the thesis, I instinctively knew that Source *wanted* what was then an academic paper to eventually be transformed into a book. I never imagined the state of our world today and the challenges we face as a result of our dismissal of the compassionate and universal values that we need now. This must be the right time.

Thank you everyone, for your support and love. I am deeply grateful.

Ciao for now.

END NOTES

Foreword

1. John W. Gardner. From a speech to McKinsey & Company (1990).

Preface

1   Ralph Waldo Emerson. *The Conduct of Life* (1860).
2   Ken Wilber. "Next Phase Integral: A Dialogue with Ken Wilber," Humanity Rising: Day 305, UbiVerse.org.
3   Hafiz, cited by Teresa Posakony. "Everything You Do Is Sacred—Hafiz," EmergingWisdom.net (March 14, 2012).

Chapter 1

1   "Sophist," Lexico.com (accessed May 28, 2020).
2   Plato (circa 370 B.C.E.). *The Republic,* translated by Desmond Lee (New York: Penguin Classics, 1955), p. 223.
3   Asociación de Emprendedores de México. "Women-Led Businesses Are More Profitable Than Those Headed by Men—Here's Why," Entrepreneur.com (March 10, 2021).
4   Pauline Graham. *Mary Parker Follett: Prophet of Management.* (Cambridge, MA.: Harvard Business School Press, 1995), p. 178.
5   Ibid.

6   Jone Johnson Lewis. "Biography of Mary Parker Follett, Management Theorist," ThoughtCo.com (May 15, 2019).

7   Mary Parker Follet. *The New State: Group Organization the Solution of Popular Government* (Mansfield Center, CT.: Martino Publishing, 2016), p. 101.

8   "Ralph Stogdill Trait Theory: Leadership Traits Theory and Skills," Biznewske.com (accessed August 18, 2021).

9   Bernard Bass and Bruce J. Avolio, editors. *Improving Organizational Effectiveness Through Transformational Leadership* (Thousand Oaks, CA.: Sage Publications, 1994).

10   Robert K. Greenleaf. *The Servant as Leader*, revised edition (Indianapolis, IN.: Greenleaf Center for Servant Leadership, 2015).

11   Ibid., referencing Hermann Hesse. *Journey to the East.* Originally published as *Die Morgenlandfahrt* in German in 1932. First English translation published 1957.

12   Ibid.

13   James Scouller. *The Three Levels of Leadership: How to Develop Your Leadership Presence, Knowhow and Skill*, second edition (Oxford, U.K.: Management Books 2000, 2016).

Chapter 2

1   Margaret J. Wheatley. *Leadership and the New Science, Learning About Organization from an Orderly Universe*, Berrett-Koehler Publishers, San Francisco 1992.

2   Zoom interview April 2021.

3   Heraclitus of Ephesus, circa 535–475 B.C.E., wrote only one publication, *On Nature.* This work was referred to by many

other writers from antiquity in their own writings, but all that remains of the original papyrus scroll are fragments. Translated in 1920 by John Burnet.

4   Richard G. Geldard. *Remembering Heraclitus* (Bel Air, CA.: Lindisfarne Books, 2000), fragment 34.

5   G. Pagnoni, M. Cekic, and Y. Guo. "'Thinking about Not-Thinking': Neural Correlates of Conceptual Processing During Zen Meditation," *PLoS ONE*, vol. 3, no. 9 (September 3, 2008), p. e3083.

6   Brainwave Entrainment Music. "Brainwave Entrainment," Brainwave-Music.com (accessed July 27, 2021).

7   Questionnaire February 2021.

8   Ralph Waldo Emerson. *Nature* (1836).

9   Ralph Waldo Emerson. *Essays: First Series* (1841).

10   Richard G. Geldard. *Remembering Heraclitus* (Bel Air, CA.: Lindisfarne Books, 2000), fragment 34.

11   Aldous Huxley. *The Perennial Philosophy* (New York: HarperPerennial Modern Classics, 2009), p. vii.

12   Ibid.

13   Sri Aurobindo. *The Life Divine* (Twin Lakes, WI.: Lotus Press, 1990), p. 78).

14   Karen Armstrong. *Islam: A Short History* (New York: Modern Library, 2002), p. 92.

15   *The Quran* (2:115). *The Holy Bible* (Luke 21:17). *Pali Canon,* the specific book and verse are unknown to me.

16   Questionnaire June 2021.

[17] Margaret Wheatly. *Leadership and the New Science: Discovering Order in a Chaotic World* (San Francisco, CA.: Berrett-Kohler Publishers, 2006), p. 143.

[18] John Jacob Gardiner. "Transactional, Transformational, and Transcendental Leadership: Metaphors Mapping the Evolution of Theory and Practice of Governance," *Leadership Review,* vol. 6 (spring 2006), p. 68.

[19] Francis H. Cook. *Hua-Yen Buddhism: The Jewel Net of Indra* (University Park, PA.: Pennsylvania State University Press, 1977), p. 3.

[20] Questionnaire January 2021.

[21] Interview essay February 2021.

Chapter 3

[1] Mohandas K. Gandhi. *Autobiography: The Story of My Experiments with Truth* (1921).

[2] Questionnaire returned November 2020.

[3] Joseph Jaworski. *Source: The Inner Path of Knowledge Creation* (San Francisco, CA.: Berrett-Koehler, 2012), p. 115.

[4] Zoom call January 2021.

[5] Zoom call April 2021.

[6] Zoom call May 2021.

[7] Brené Brown. *Dare to Lead: Brave Work. Tough Conversations. Whole Hearts* (New York: Penguin Random House, 2018), p. 12.

[8] Questionnaire returned January 2021.

[9] Zoom call February 2021.

[10] Email July 20, 2021.

[11] Questionnaire February 2021.

[12] Zoom call January 2021.

[13] Zoom call April 2021.

[14] Questionnaire November 2020.

[15] Zoom call April 2021.

[16] Questionnaire February 2021.

[17] Questionnaire February 2021.

[18] Zoom call February 2021.

[19] Zoom call March 2021.

[20] Questionnaire February 2021.

Chapter 4

[1] Joseph Jaworski. *Source: The Inner Path of Knowledge Creation* (San Francisco, CA.: Berrett-Koehler, 2012), p. 163.

[2] "Gaia Hypothesis," Wikipedia (accessed September 20, 2020).

[3] Questionnaire January 2021.

[4] From a motivational poster.

[5] B. Alan Wallace. *Tibetan Buddhism From the Ground Up, A Practical Approach for Modern Life*, Wisdom Publications, 1993. p. 51.

[6] David Lynch. *Enlightenment Now* (2013).

[7] Questionnaire February 2021.

[8] Written in interview January 2021

[9] *New Catholic Bible* (Catholic Book Publishing Corps, 2019).

[10] Cynthia Bourgeault. *The Heart of Centering Prayer: Nondual Christianity in Theory and Practice* (Boulder, CO.: Shambhala, 2016), p. 5.

11   Sue McGreevey. "Eight Weeks to a Better Brain," Harvard Gazette (January 21, 2011).

12   Sara Lazar. Various studies conducted by the Lazar Lab for Meditation Research at Massachusetts General Hospital.

13   Paramahansa Yogananda. *The Second Coming of Christ: The Resurrection of the Christ Within You*, Self-Realization Fellowship, September 2004. p. 495.

14   Joseph Jaworski. Zoom call April 2021.

15   Eckhart Tolle. *The Power of Now: A Guide to Spiritual Enlightenment* (Novato, CA.: New World Library, 2010), pp. 20–1.

16   Zoom call January 2021.

17   Rainer Maria Rilke. "Fear Not the Strangeness," *Letters to a Young Poet*, translated by Stephen Mitchell (New York: Vintage Books, 1986).

18   *The Bible. International Standard Version.* Copyright © 1995–2014 by ISV Foundation. Used by permission of Davidson Press, LLC.

19   European Science Foundation. "How Mirror Neurons Allow Us to Learn and Socialize by Going Through the Motions in the Head," ScienceDaily.com (December 21, 2008.

20   Questionnaire January 2021.

21   Dalai Lama. *Ethics for the New Millennium, reissue edition* (New York: Riverhead Books, 2001), p. 234.

22   Paramahansa Yogananda. *The Bhagavad Gita: Royal Science of God-Realization* (Los Angeles, CA.: Self-Realization Fellowship, 1995), p. 7.

23   Zoom call May 2021.

24 Zoom call March 2021.
25 Zoom call April 2021.
26 Zoom call February 2021.
27 Zoom call January 2021.
28 Zoom call March 2021.

Chapter 5

1 Jean Houston. Weekend workshop in Los Angeles 2001.
2 Jean Houston. "The 'Future of God' Debate," *Huffington Post* (May 10, 2010, updated November 17, 2011).
3 Ralph Waldo Emerson. *Heroism* (1841).

Epilogue

1 Zoom call in March 2021.
2 B. Alan Wallace. *Buddhism with an Attitude: The Tibetan Seven-Point Mind Training,* reprint edition (Ithaca, N.Y.: Snow Lion Publications, 2003), p. 80.

ABOUT THE INTERVIEW SUBJECTS

Paris Ackrill, Cofounder of Avalon Wellbeing (Yorkshire, U.K.), is the partner to Roger Tempest and mother of Aya. Paris is a wellbeing guide dedicated to the path of spiritual and personal growth through a holistic and embodied approach. Paris creates space helping people find freedom, alignment and lightness in their being through retreats and events at Avalon using an alchemy of sound, energy work, meditation, movement meditation, breathing techniques, and spiritual ceremony. She has studied with a wonderful family of teachers including global movement activist Shiva Rea, sound master Yantara Jiro, the Modern Mystery School and Brazilian spiritual teachers Chandra and Surya Lacombe. Paris believes in creating peace within for a more harmonious world. Her mission is to share the joy, lightness, freedom, creativity, and hunger to be of help. Avalon seeks to provide space for exploration into new fields of reality. Paris can be reached at: www.avalonwellbeing.com.

Esperide Ananas Ametista, is a sociopsychologist, energy therapist, and spiritual facilitator, overseeing many of the operational communications for Damanhur, the Temples of Humankind in Italy. Born in Milan, Esperide studied and worked in several countries before moving to the beautiful

Piedmont Valley where the Federation of Spiritual Communities of Damanhur is located. Her first job was for the European Parliament at age twenty-two. Since then, she has been a consultant for many companies and organizations looking for a more conscious approach to their work.

Esperide attended the Spiritual Healing School at Damanhur and perfected her abilities to connect to transcendent fields of information and energy through oracle practices and past-life research. She teaches and conducts healing sessions all over the world, both in person and over the internet. She is the author of several books connected to Damanhur's spiritual vision and healing practices. Esperide can be reached at: www.thetemples.org.

Catherine Butler is the founder and owner of At the Chapel, a restaurant, retreat center, bakery, and wine store in Somerset in the English countryside. At the Chapel provides cultural programs, loving hospitality, and scenic beauty to visitors from around the world. Catherine can be reached at www.atthechapel.co.uk or at Catherine@atthechapel.co.uk.

Jude Currivan, Ph.D., Cofounder of WholeWorld-View, is a cosmologist, planetary healer, and author, and previously one of the most senior U.K. businesswomen working globally. She has experienced multidimensional realities since early childhood, travelled to over eighty countries and worked with wisdom keepers from many traditions. She holds a Ph.D. in archaeology from the University of Reading in the United Kingdom, researching ancient cosmologies, and a master's degree in physics from Oxford University, specializing in cosmology and quantum physics.

Jude integrates leading-edge science, consciousness research, and universal wisdom teachings into a wholistic worldview, underpinning her work to enable and facilitate transformational and emergent resolutions to our collective planetary issues. The international author of six nonfiction books, including best-selling and Nautilus Award-winning *The Cosmic Hologram: Information at the Center of Creation*, the first book in her Transformation trilogy. She is currently writing book two: *Gaia: Her-Story*.

In 2010, Jude was presented with a CIRCLE Award by WON Buddhism International for her "outstanding contribution towards planetary healing and expanding new forms of consciousness." She is a member of the Evolutionary Leaders Circle and in 2017 cofounded WholeWorld-View to empower the understanding, experiencing, and embodying of unity awareness in service to conscious evolution. Jude can be reached through her website: www.judecurrivan.com.

Patty DeDominic is a business coach to executives and entrepreneurs. After decades of building her own multimillion-dollar enterprise, Patty became an angel investor, executive business coach, and business consultant. Named CEO of the Year by *LA Business Journal,* she founded and acquired companies that placed over 250,000 people in American jobs, the United States and Japanese space programs, programmers in the Philippines, and government strategists in Jamaica for the United Nations Development Program. Patty has received lifetime achievement awards from two U.S. presidents. She holds corporate governance certification from University of California, Berkeley, and was trained in leadership and negotiations at Harvard University.

Active in the community and philanthropy, some of Patty's chairmanships include the National Association of Women Business Owners and CompassionCantWait.org, an organization that helps families when their children have been diagnosed with critical illness. Patty worked closely with Dr. Jane Goodall, as board member and chair of governance, to expand Roots & Shoots, a network of kids making a difference for their communities, the environment, and animals, to over sixty countries.

Patty can be reached at: www.dedominic.com

James Garrison, Ph.D., is founder and president of Ubiquity University. He comes to this having served as founding president of Wisdom University, which he led from 2005–2012, after which it transitioned into Ubiquity. He has spent his entire professional life in executive leadership, including as founder and president of both the Gorbachev Foundation/USA from 1992–1995 and State of the World Forum from 1995–2004 with Mikhail Gorbachev serving as convening chairman. He attended the University of Santa Clara for his bachelor's degree in history, Harvard University for his master's degree in the history of religion, and Cambridge University for his doctorate degree in philosophical theology. He has written seven books, beginning with *The Plutonium Culture* in 1979 to the current book he is writing on *Climate Change and the Primordial*

Mind. He taught regularly throughout his tenure at Wisdom University on Greek philosophy, world history, and the philosophical implications of global warming. He continues to teach at Ubiquity. Jim can be reached through the website www.UbiquityUniversity.org.

Joseph Jaworski has devoted much of his life to exploring the deeper dimensions of transformational leadership. He is the author of the best-selling books *Source: The Inner Path of Leadership, Presence: The Inner Path of Knowledge Creation,* and *Synchronicity: An Exploration of Profound Change.* As founder and chairman of Generon International and Global Leadership Initiative, Joseph advises CEOs and senior executives in Fortune 500 companies. He specializes in the design and execution of large-scale organizational change, as well as strategy formation and implementation. He is a pioneer and prominent thought leader in the discipline of strategic foresight, enabling leaders to deepen their capacity for tactical and strategic insight. From his ranch just outside of Austin, Texas, Joseph remains actively working with Generon clients and enjoys spending time practicing qigong and meditation and communing with nature.

Peter Matthies is a former venture capitalist and founder of the Conscious Business Institute (CBI). Before CBI, Peter was a principal for a leading global private equity and venture capital firm Apax Partners & Co., and for b-business partners, a $1 billion pan-European VC fund.

The Conscious Business Institute provides a measurable, scalable, academically validated system for building more inspiring, conscious organizations. CBI's programs have been applied by more than 28,000 professionals in organizations from one to 150,000 employees, including Starbucks, BMW Group, Siemens, Allianz Global Investors, Intel, and others.

Peter cofounded an internet technology company and started his career at Accenture in Germany. He has published two books and several dozen articles on business, finance, leadership, martial arts, and technology. He's a faculty member of the Goethe Business School in Frankfurt, Germany, fellow of the World Business Academy, serves as a global advisor of the Climate Prosperity Alliance, and is on the board of several for-profit and nonprofit organizations.

Peter lives in Santa Barbara, California, and gets a kick out of aikido, capoeira, sailing, and a good dance with his wife. He can be reached at: www.consciousbusinessinstitute.com.

Peter Merry, Ph.D., is Cofounding Chief Innovation Officer at Ubiquity University. He is one of the world's top experts on transformative leadership, working in and across different sectors, training government ministers, CEOs, and civil society leaders. His experience includes facilitating integral change processes in multinational corporations and government ministries, and in multistakeholder initiatives with global stakeholders. He has also spent many years in the not-for-profit sector. He is a recognized expert in the field of futureproof learning, evolutionary systems dynamics, and integral leadership.

Peter had his first book, *Evolutionary Leadership* (2005), published in English and Dutch. His second *Why Work?* (2019)

was on designing work for people and planet. His third was *Leading from the Field* (2020). He has a master's degree in human ecology from Edinburgh University and a doctorate from Ubiquity's Wisdom School on evolution theory. For more information, see https://petermerry.org.

Stephan Rechtschaffen, M.D., is a physician, author, and founder of Blue Spirit Costa Rica, the Nosara Longevity Center, and the Omega Institute for Holistic Studies in New York. As a visionary entrepreneur, he has developed financially thriving organizations in areas that otherwise require donations or outside funding. He regularly consults for socially integrative organizations focused on creating positive, self-sustaining changes in the world aligned with inner wisdom.

As a physician and teacher, he created the Nosara Longevity Center at Blue Spirit Costa Rica for people to learn and experience integrative approaches to wellbeing, managing time, stress reduction, and longevity—where people attend week-long or longer-stay programs to restore health and vitality with a balanced inner and outer lifestyle. He's the author of *Timeshifting,* which focuses on how to reduce stress in a crazy world fixated on going faster.

Stephan's latest passion-project is a major venture in Costa Rica to reverse the global use of pesticides through natural treatments and other initiatives to reduce climate change impact. Stephan can be reached through the website www.bluespiritcostarica.com.

John Renesch is a pioneer in the field of conscious leadership. He started his career as a serial entrepreneur, starting his first business at eighteen years of age in the mid-1950s. He continued on this path, serving as founder or cofounder of companies in the real estate, investment securities, and event production industries, until he experienced a personal transformation in the mid-1970s. He has since published fourteen books and approximately 1,000 articles on paradigm shifts, social change, and conscious leadership, including *The Great Growing Up,* which received the 2013 Grand Prize for Non-Fiction from the Next Generation Indie Books Awards.

In addition to his writings, John has served as a professional consultant and executive coach, as well as a well-traveled keynote speaker who has presented challenging questions and observations to audiences in Tokyo, Seoul, Brussels, London, Sao Paulo, Porto Alegre, Zurich, Amsterdam, Port-of-Spain, Caracas, Gold Coast, Brisbane, Budapest, and many U.S. cities.

For over twenty years, he has published a free monthly newsletter, *John Renesch's Mini-Keynote,* which includes short editorials. Most recently John helped found the Conscious Leadership Guild, an international membership association for professionals who focus on conscious leadership as the core of their work.

John's can be contacted by email john@renesch.com (San Francisco).

Juliet Rohde-Brown, Ph.D., is a licensed clinical psychologist in Santa Barbara and Carpinteria, California. She is chair of the Depth Psychology: Integrative Therapy and Healing Practices doctoral specialization at Pacifica Graduate Institute. She is also an interspiritual mentor with the Spiritual Paths Institute and has led retreats and workshops and spoken at conferences internationally.

She is the author of *Imagine Forgiveness* and her peer-reviewed journal articles and guided visualizations have been distributed worldwide. She is on the board of Restorative Justice Resources and the Sacred Earth Foundation, and she is past president of Imagery International. She is past advocacy representative for the Santa Barbara County Psychological Association as well. Juliet has had a meditation practice since the early 1990s and enjoys the arts. She lives in Carpinteria, California, with her husband, artist James Paul Brown.

Juliet can be reached at www.pacifica.edu.

Peter Russell, M.A., D.C.S., is on the faculty of the Institute of Noetic Sciences, a fellow of the World Business Academy and the Findhorn Foundation, and an honorary member of the Club of Budapest. He studied mathematics and theoretical physics at Cambridge University. Fascinated by the mysteries of the human mind, he changed to experimental psychology, traveling to India to study meditation and eastern philosophy. Upon his return, he took up the first research post ever offered in Britain on the psychology of meditation. In addition, he has a post-graduate degree in computer science.

Peter was one of the first people to introduce human potential seminars into the corporate field. Clients have included IBM, Apple, American Express, Barclays Bank, Shell Oil, and British Petroleum. His newest book is *Letting Go of*

Nothing: Relax Your Mind and Discover the Wonder of Your True Nature. His other books include *The TM Technique, The Upanishads, The Brain Book, The Creative Manager, The Consciousness Revolution, Waking Up in Time, The Global Brain, Seeds of Awakening,* and *From Science to God.*

A revolutionary futurist, Peter has been a keynote speaker at many international conferences. His principal interest is the deeper, spiritual significance of our times. Peter can be reached through his website www.peterrussell.com.

Bishop Heather Shea is the CEO and Spiritual Director for the United Palace of Spiritual Arts in New York City. She is a member of the Evolutionary Leaders Circle, a group committed to collectively inspire, support, and serve conscious evolution for humanity. Heather has partnered with CEOs of the Fortune 100 and other global organizations to transform their organizational strategies and cultures to achieve business results.

After a career in the theater as an actor, singer, and dancer, Heather moved into the business arena. She has played senior roles in organizations that include Bridgewater, J. P Morgan, and Accenture. Prior to joining the Palace, she was director of leadership for the Clinton Foundation. Earlier, Heather was president and CEO of the Tom Peters Group, a global leadership consultancy.

Among numerous articles and columns, Heather is the author of two books: *Dance Lessons: Six Steps to Great Partnerships in Business and Life,* coauthored with Chip Bell, and *Online Learning Today: Strategies That Work,* coauthored with John Fogarty.

Heather studied at the University of South Florida and the Kellogg Graduate School of Management at Northwestern University. She became an ordained Interfaith minister in June 2015 and is pursuing a doctorate in transformational leadership. Heather can be contacted at www.unitedpalace.org.

Agapi Stassinopoulos is a best-selling author and speaker, inspiring audiences around the world. In her book *Unbinding the Heart: A Dose of Greek Wisdom, Generosity, and Unconditional Love,* she shares the wisdom from her adventures and experiences. In her book *Wake Up to the Joy of You: 52 Meditations and Practices for a Calmer, Happier Life,* she inspires readers to let go of what doesn't work and to create the lives they really want. Agapi was trained in London at the Royal Academy of Dramatic Art and received her master's degree in psychology from the University of Santa Monica. Her books on the Greek archetypes, *Gods and Goddesses in Love* and *Conversations with the Goddesses,* were turned into PBS specials. She conducts workshops for Thrive Global, a company founded by her sister, Arianna Huffington, to help change the way we work and live. Agapi has spoken and conducted meditations at many organizations including L'Oréal, LinkedIn, Pandora, Nike, and Google, among others. She divides her time between Athens, Greece, and Los Angeles. You can reach Agapi at www.wakeuptothejoyofyou.com.

Susan Taylor is a transformational coach and consultant who has worked with some of the most renowned thought leaders in the domains of emotional, spiritual, and leadership intelligence for more than twenty-five years. She helps clients fulfill their deeper purpose by fostering creative and inspiring business environments that support people to learn, grow, and thrive while delivering extraordinary results. Susan possesses a deep passion and expertise in dialogue—specifically, Bohm Dialogue. This has proven to lead to new and deeper understandings, resulting in profound transformations.

As CEO and Cofounder of Generon International, Susan works with C-level leaders and teams from organizations of all sizes. She serves in a coaching and facilitative capacity, leading workshops, trainings, and wilderness retreats, as well as deep one-one-one work. As an ongoing contributor to *Forbes,* Susan writes on topics based in human consciousness, and she serves on the board of the Conscious Leadership Guild.

Susan continues to practice and teach meditation and qigong and has a strong connection to nature while living on Hilton Head Island, South Carolina.

She can be contacted at www.tayloredwisdom.com.

Roger Tempest is the thirty-second generation of Tempest family members to be the custodian of the Broughton Hall Estate in Yorkshire, England. At the center of this sanctuary is Avalon, a newly formed wellbeing center specializing in transformational work in terms of personal development of the mind, body, and spirit. This new retreat center has hosted groups varying from Hoffman Process, Path of Love, Diamond, and ConsciousCafe to mental health gatherings and visits by Guatemalan Mayan elders. Roger's past experience came from being in newspaper management (*Today* and *The Observer*) to owning and developing a radio station to publishing interests. He founded Rural Solutions, a U.K. rural regeneration company. He established a multiple award-winning rural business park and won the U.K. Restoration of the Year Award for Aldourie Castle Estate. His entrepreneurial activities also range to being the executive chairman of Rural Concepts Group with interests in major projects in Libya, the Arab Emirates, the United Kingdom, and Oman. He is a trustee of three charities. His main sense of purpose is creating projects that are a force for good and being of service to a new reshaped world. Roger is also father to Aya and partner of Paris Ackrill.

Contact Roger at www.BroughtonHall.co.uk.

Wildrik Timmerman is the cofounder (with Wouter Tavecchio) of the Mandali Foundation and the Mandali Retreat Center in the Northern Lakes Region of Italy. Both from the Netherlands, he and Wouter also cofounded Q-Dance, a music festival company, prior to visioning, building, and creating Mandali. Individually and together, they also are founders and collaborators with a number of other transformational centers and programs in the Netherlands. Wildrik can be reached at www.Mandali.org.

Anne-Marie Voorhoeve is the founder, director and strategic connector of the Hague Center. She is a strategist, social alchemist, social architect, innovative cocreator, experienced facilitator, and expert in meshworking. She focuses on the integral transformation of society into a sustainable world. Anne-Marie has international experience with communities, businesses, networks, organizations, technology providers, groups of politicians, and NGOs. She enjoys designing and supporting complex multistakeholder projects that commit to meaningful and ambitious goals, for example: the Offices of the Future development with the Wheel of Cocreation. Certified in Spiral Dynamics integral, Art of Hosting, SQ21 spiritual intelligence and ECO-Intention, she uses social technologies like the World Café, Spiral Dynamics, Open Space, U Theory, Appreciative Inquiry, Generative Dialogue, Holacracy, Systemic Constellation Work, and Meshworking to enable large groups of people to efficiently interact and gain access to their collective intelligence, wisdom and consciousness.

Chief Creative Director for the International Club of Budapest (COB) and president of COB Netherlands, Anne-Marie is a core team member of Integral City Meshworks Ltd. and founder/partner of Integral City Netherlands.

Anne-Marie can be reached through www.linkedin.com/in/annemarievoorhoeve.

Roger Walsh, M.D., Ph.D., D.H.L., graduated from Queensland University with degrees in psychology, physiology, neuroscience, and medicine before coming to the U.S. as a Fulbright Scholar. He is now at the University of California at Irvine where he is a professor of psychiatry, philosophy, and anthropology, as well as a professor in the religious studies program.

He is the author of several books including *Essential Spirituality* (with a foreword by the Dalai Lama*)* and *Paths Beyond Ego.* His articles include editing: *Gifts from of a Course* *in Miracles*. Dr. Walsh also facilitates retreats around the world. He can be reached through: www.drrogerwalsh.com.

Judi Weisbart is the founder and president of A Busy Woman Consulting, helping for-profit and nonprofit organizations create events, raise funds, and develop business. The overriding vision of the business is to create mission-driven events and strategies that form a bond of trust between the organizations and the donors. Judi has served and worked with dozens of organizations, individuals, and businesses throughout the southern California region and abroad, such as the Women's Festivals, Martin Luther King Day Celebration, and political fundraisers.

As a thirty-five-year resident of Santa Barbara, California, Judi has deep knowledge of and connections to the myriad subcommunities: social, faith, arts, education, and business. She has received several prestigious awards for her commitment to creating a better world. She is also an accomplished artist, whose works have been widely shown. Judi has a passion for social justice, peace, compassion, and beauty. In all her artwork, her purpose is to help create a better world. Judi has said that the voice inside her tells her to be the change she wants to see.

Judi may be contacted at https://jweisbart.com.

Claudia Welss is a citizen scientist in the power of unconditional love and Board Chairman, Institute of Noetic Sciences (IONS), founded by Apollo 14 astronaut and the sixth man to walk on the Moon, Captain Edgar Mitchell. Previously she was at the University of California, Berkeley Haas School of

Business, pioneering social responsibility and sustainability curriculum for global corporations. She chairs the IONS board science committee and is on the boards of HeartMath's Global Coherence Initiative and Space for Humanity ("To Space, for Earth").

Claudia is Founding Chair of the Invest in Yourself Working Group at Nexus Global, bringing practical consciousness research to NextGen philanthropists, impact investors, social entrepreneurs, activists, and influencers focused on global transformation, and a cofounder of the Global Coherence Pulse, a social experiment in collective coherence backed by science. She founded NextNow Collaboratory, described by the director of MIT's Center for Collective Intelligence as an example of a "new kind of collective intelligence."

Claudia is an executive producer of the award-winning *Edgar Mitchell Overview Effect Virtual Reality Experience* (2020) and the upcoming film *The Space Less Traveled* (2022). Her essay, "Humanity's Change of Heart" appears in the Evolutionary Leaders Circle 2020 Gold Nautilus Award-winning anthology *Our Moment of Choice*, published by Beyond Words/Simon and Schuster (2021). Claudia can be contacted through www.noetic.org.

Judith Skutch Whitson is Cofounder and Board Chairwoman, Inner Peace Foundation. Publishers of *A Course in Miracles,* whose first edition was published in 1975. Over three million volumes of the book have been circulated worldwide and translated into more than twenty-five languages to date. Judith was a founding member of the Institute of

Noetic Sciences and the Fetzer Institute. Today, she lives in northern California.

Diane Marie Williams is Founder and President of the Source of Synergy Foundation, an organization committed to consciously synergizing individuals and organizations by tapping into the infinite source of the collective potential to serve as a positive force for global transformation. She was the initiator, with Deepak Chopra, of the Evolutionary Leaders Circle and is one of the authors of the book *Our Moment of Choice: Evolutionary Visions and Hope for the Future.*

Diane initiated the formation of the NGO Committee on Spirituality, Values, and Global Concerns at the United Nations in New York where she served as the first chairperson. She also served as their cochair and cofounding member at the United Nations in Geneva, where it originated. She is a founding member of the Council of the Spiritual Caucus at the United Nations in New York and was the cocreator of the Sacred Place at the United Nations World Summit on Sustainable Development. She was a U.N. Representative for the Tribal Link Foundation for over a decade and was the Director of International and U.N. Affairs at the Interfaith Center of New York; as well as International Consultant and U.N. Representative for the Temple of Understanding. She is the founder of the Contact Card, which connects homeless individuals to food, shelter, job counseling, and other free services in New York City. She has won a number of awards, including the Spirit of the United Nations Award, the Golden Rule award at the UN, and the PEMAC Peace Award.

Diane can be contacted at www.sourceofsynergyfoundation. org.

ABOUT THE AUTHOR

Shawne Mitchell, M.A., is an author and speaker recognized as an expert in bridging conscious living with a spiritual lifestyle. A thought leader, social alchemist, and consultant, she holds a master's degree in consciousness studies from the University of Philosophical Research in Los Angeles, California. She also holds a bachelor's degree in communications from the University of Washington in Seattle, Washington.

Shawne has been a practitioner of Transcendental Meditation for over forty years. After college, she lived and worked in Brazil for the Brazilian National Institute of Space Research. Moving to Los Angeles in 1984, Shawne was part of the startup for the Small Luxury Hotels Association. After a career as a realtor and feng shui author in West Los Angeles and Santa Barbara, California, she began working with retreat centers in the areas of marketing and business development—most recently at Mandali Retreat Center in Italy. Shawne moved to Italy and returned to the United States in 2020 as a result of the coronavirus pandemic and lockdown.

Shawne is also a former community group leader for the Institute of Noetic Sciences; a member of the Santa Barbara Evolutionary Leaders and the Conscious Business Synergy Circle, groups committed to collectively inspire, support, and serve the conscious evolution for humanity, and a current member of the global Conscious Leadership Guild.

The natural sharing of her wisdom, combined with retreat center expertise, and insights from her travels and experiences, has evolved into an international consulting practice.

Shawne has taught and facilitated retreats and conferences throughout the world. Her previously published books include *Exploring Feng Shui: Ancient Secrets and Modern Insight for Love, Joy, and Abundance* (New Page Books), *Simple Feng Shui: Ancient Principles to Bring Love, Joy, and Prosperity into Your Life* (Random House), and *Home Sanctuaries: Creating Sacred Spaces, Altars, and Shrines* (Soul Style Press). Her books have been translated into several international languages.

Shawne is the mother of two grown sons and is currently an antevasin nomad.

Visit her website: www.shawnemitchell.com.